Aging in America

Aging in America

The Federal Government's Role

Congressional Quarterly Inc.
1414 22nd Street N.W.
Washington, D.C. 20037

Congressional Quarterly Inc.

Congressional Quarterly Inc., an editorial research service and publishing company, serves clients in the fields of news, education, business, and government. It combines Congressional Quarterly's specific coverage of Congress, government, and politics with the more general subject range of an affiliated service, Editorial Research Reports.

Congressional Quarterly publishes the *Congressional Quarterly Weekly Report* and a variety of books, including college political science textbooks under the CQ Press imprint and public affairs paperbacks on developing issues and events. CQ also publishes information directories and reference books on the federal government, national elections, and politics, including the *Guide to Congress*, the *Guide to the U.S. Supreme Court*, the *Guide to U.S. Elections*, *Politics in America*, and *Congress A to Z: CQ's Ready Reference Encyclopedia*. The *CQ Almanac,* a compendium of legislation for one session of Congress, is published each year. *Congress and the Nation*, a record of government for a presidential term, is published every four years.

CQ publishes *The Congressional Monitor,* a daily report on current and future activities of congressional committees, and several newsletters including *Congressional Insight,* a weekly analysis of congressional action, and *Campaign Practices Reports,* a semimonthly update on campaign laws.

An electronic online information system, Washington Alert, provides immediate access to CQ's databases of legislative action, votes, schedules, profiles, and analyses.

Printed in the United States of America

Library of Congress Cataloging-in-Publication Data

Aging in America.

    1. Aged--Government policy--United States. 2. Old age assistance--United States. 3. Aged--Care--Government policy--United States. I. Congressional Quarterly, inc.
HV1461.A54   1989   362.6′042   88-28539
ISBN 0-87187-501-2

Editor: Colleen McGuiness
Writers: Robert K. Landers, Julie Rovner
Cover: Kathleen Sims

Congressional Quarterly Inc.

Andrew Barnes *Chairman and President*
Wayne P. Kelley *Publisher*
Neil Skene *Executive Editor*
John J. Coyle *General Manager*
Robert E. Cuthriell *Director of Development*
Robert C. Hur *General Counsel*

Book Division

Robert C. Hur *Director*

David R. Tarr *Director, Book Department*
John L. Moore *Assistant Director*
Joanne D. Daniels *Director, CQ Press*
Mary W. Cohn *Associate Editor*
Nancy A. Lammers *Managing Editor*
Carolyn Goldinger *Senior Editor*
Margaret Seawell Benjaminson *Project Editor*
Ann Davies *Project Editor*
Colleen McGuiness *Project Editor*
Jane S. Gilligan *Production Editor*
Kerry V. Kern *Production Editor*
Noell H. Sottile *Production Editor*
Linda White *Administrative Assistant*

Kathryn C. Suárez *Director, Book Marketing*
Jacqueline A. Davey *Library Marketing Manager*
Ellen Loerke *Assistant College Marketing Manager*
Leslie Brenowitz *Administrative Assistant*

Production

I. D. Fuller *Production Manager*
Maceo Mayo *Assistant Production Manager*

Table of Contents

Aging in America

The Elderly

There is a wide gap between the common perception of what old age is like and what it really is. Most of America's 29.8 million elderly people are not poor. Most are not disabled. And most of those who are disabled are not in nursing homes.

"The impression that the overwhelming issue with older people is being institutionalized and being comatose [is] just a wild distortion," said Lydia Bronte, coeditor of *Our Aging Society.* Institutionalization and disability may be "a very serious problem" for a minority of elderly people, she said, "but 85 percent of everybody over 65 is really in pretty good shape."

What it means to be old in America is a matter of increasing importance, because the elderly here represent not only a population greater than all of Canada's but a rapidly growing share of the total U.S. population. At the turn of the century, only 4 percent of Americans were sixty-five or older. By 1950, that percentage had doubled, and by 1986 it had tripled. Since the proportion of young people has been declining, the whole American population is "aging"—a trend that will have a profound impact on society.

The rapid growth in the elderly population is due mainly to increases in the annual number of births before 1921, but greater longevity also plays a part. A person born at the turn of the century could expect to live an average of forty-nine years; now, life expectancy at birth is seventy-one years for males and seventy-eight years for females. Moreover, persons who reach old age are living longer, mainly because of reduced death rates from major cardiovascular diseases. The life expectancy of someone who reached age sixty-five in 1900 was twelve years; in 1950, it was fourteen years. Now, life expectancy at age sixty-five is fifteen years for men and nineteen years for women.

Poverty once was a common fact of elderly life. "In the past most of the elderly suffered from serious economic deprivation," wrote Brandeis University economist James H. Schulz in *The Economics of Aging.* "Their incomes were inadequate, and inflation exacerbated the situation by reducing real incomes and eroding savings. Most people knew that the aged were one of the largest poverty groups in the country. Today the situation is greatly improved, due in large part to our nation's very positive response to the past economic plight of the elderly."

"There are, indeed, many elderly who live on the edge of economic survival—too many," wrote Stephen Crystal in his book, *America's Old Age Crisis.* "But grinding poverty is far from being universal or even typical. Most of the elderly poor have been poor most of their lives. Retirement can be accompanied by a significant decline in earnings, but the middle-class elderly usually can maintain a middle-class standard of living."

Government programs have helped to improve the elderly's economic condition in recent decades. Some of them, like Social Security, which has been indexed to inflation, and Medicare, the federal health care program for the aged, are specifically designed to help the elderly. Others are broader in scope: Medicaid, the federal-state welfare program that finances health services for the poor; the Supplemental Security Income program to assist the elderly, blind, and disabled; and the food stamp program. The elderly also have been helped by increases in real wages and the spread of private pension plans.

Not only are there fewer elderly poor—3.5 million in 1986, 1.3 million fewer than in 1970—but fewer of the elderly are poor—12.4 percent in 1986, about half what the percentage was in 1970 and only one-third of the 1959 level. By contrast, 19.8 percent of children under eighteen—and 42.7 percent of black children—live in poverty. Only one in ten of the nation's impoverished population is elderly.

Nevertheless, there is a "hard core" of elderly poor. Most are unmarried black women with limited education. Many of them live alone. Extended-family living rescues some of the elderly from poverty, but about one in four unmarried old people dwelling alone is poor. The fact that most are women has a lot to do with it. "Women in general, when they become widowed, often lose the private pension income of their husband, and certainly their Social Security [income] is reduced from when their husband was alive," explained Cynthia M. Taeuber, chief of the age and sex statistics branch in the Census Bureau's population division.

The impoverished elderly, as well as the elderly population in general, is now predominantly female. Until about 1950, roughly half the elderly were men. But women now tend to live longer than men, and elderly women outnumber elderly men by a ratio of 3-to-2. The imbalance increases with age. Among people eighty-five and older, there are only about forty men for every one hundred women. Indeed, because most of the elderly, especially those over age seventy-five, are women, Taeuber and demographer Jacob S. Siegel noted in an essay in *Our Aging Society: Paradox and Promise* that "the health, social, and economic problems of the elderly may be viewed as mostly the problems of women."

Today's Elderly

Just as most people sixty-five or over are not poor, so most are not disabled, physically or mentally. "Most men and women over 65 today are vigorous, healthy, mentally alert, and still young in outlook," Alan Pifer and Lydia Bronte wrote in the introduction to *Our Aging Society*.

"You could . . . say that being 'elderly' doesn't really start until you're something like 80 or 85," Bronte said. "I think it's a misnomer to call somebody 65 or 70 'elderly.' " Although it is often assumed that increased longevity means additional years of "old age," Bronte said, "What has really happened is that . . . you've added more years to the middle period of adult vitality."

Less than one-fourth of the entire elderly populace—and only one-seventh of those aged from sixty-five to seventy-four—were disabled in 1985. And of the 6.3 million disabled elderly, only 2.6 million—less than 10 percent of all the elderly—were "severely" disabled (that is, in need of help with three or more of these everyday activities: eating, going to the toilet, bathing, dressing, getting in and out of bed, and getting around inside).

Most of the elderly who are disabled are not in nursing homes. Only about 21 percent of the disabled elderly were in nursing homes in 1985. Even among the "severely" disabled, fewer than half were in nursing homes. Most care of the elderly in the United States is provided by the family. "Families devote enormous time and energy to the care of elderly relatives, often at considerable emotional and physical cost," wrote Alice M. Rivlin and Joshua M. Wiener of the Brookings Institution in their book, *Caring for the Disabled Elderly: Who Will Pay?* "The strong role of the family in long-term care runs counter to the myth that American families, who supposedly took care of their aging relatives at home 'in the good old days,' are now 'dumping' them in nursing homes. In fact, in the past, few families cared for an elderly parent because relatively few people lived long enough to experience a prolonged period of disability."

That is not the case any longer. Now, large numbers of people, mostly women, are reaching very old age, and more and more families are being affected. By one estimate, the proportion of fifty-year-old women with living mothers increased from 37 percent in 1940 to 65 percent in 1980. This phenomenon—of a large majority of middle-aged women having living mothers—is "new to human experience," Siegel and Taeuber noted.

Living Independently

Most elderly Americans express a strong preference for living independently—that is, with only a spouse or, if necessary, alone. This is not a new trend. According to a 1957 National Opinion Research Center survey, only 26 percent of people sixty and older felt that "older people sharing a home with their grown children" was "a good idea." Similar surveys in 1976 and 1978 found only 23 percent of the

older respondents approving of the idea. A 1986 Louis Harris survey of elderly people who live alone found that 86 percent wanted to continue to do so, instead of living with relatives or friends or in an institution.

In recent decades, more and more of the elderly have been able to follow their preference and live independently. In 1960,

---

Statistics on the Elderly

Number of Americans sixty-five or older—29,835,000

Percentage of Americans sixty-five or older in 1950—8
   In 1987—12
   Projected for 2030—21

Life expectancy at birth:
   In 1900—male, forty-eight years; female, fifty-one
   In 1987—male, seventy-one years; female, seventy-eight

Ratio of women to men:
   Sixty-five and older—3:2
   Eighty-five and older—5:2

Percentage of elderly below poverty level—12.4
   Of children under eighteen—19.8

Percentage of elderly in nursing homes—4.6

Living alone:
   Percentage of noninstitutionalized elderly—30
   Number of elderly men—2 million
   Number of elderly women—6.5 million

Percentage living alone who prefer living alone—86

fewer than two out of ten noninstitutionalized elderly people lived alone; now, about three in ten do so. The proportion of the noninstitutionalized elderly living with their spouses has remained about the same, but increasingly they live *only* with their spouses. The proportion living with both spouse and others fell from 15 percent in 1960 to 8 percent in 1984, according to a Congressional Budget Office (CBO) study.

"There has been relatively little change in the proportion of elderly men living alone or with other family members," Siegel and Taeuber observed. Now, as in the 1960s, only about 15 percent of elderly men live alone; more than 80 percent live with family members. By contrast, there has been a sharp increase in the proportion of women living alone. About 40 percent of elderly women now live alone; less than a third did so in 1965. The trend is especially pronounced among women seventy-five and older; more than half of them now live alone.

A key reason is financial. The real incomes of the elderly have increased substantially in recent decades, thanks largely to increases in real wages, improvements in Social Security benefits, and the growth of private pension programs. More of the elderly can afford to live independently.

"For most of the elderly who maintain their own households, separation from relatives entails little economic or physical hardship," the CBO study said. "Indeed, ... the trend away from extended family residence can, overall, be counted as improvement in the quality of life for older Americans."

Independence is "a strongly held value, [and] we don't give it up when we get old. We assert it and reassert it as a sign that we're not really old and don't want to be protected," said William G. Bell, a Florida State University gerontologist who turned seventy-four in August 1988. "Both the adult children and the parent prefer that we live separately. But that does not mean that our relationships are poor. It's just that the shared roof has a lot of negatives."

Nearly three-fourths of elderly people living alone have children, and most live near them and see them frequently. Among independent elderly parents aged sixty-five to seventy-four, almost seven in ten live near one of their children, and among those aged eighty-five or older, nearly eight in ten do.

Independent living by the elderly "is likely to become increasingly prevalent over the next half century and beyond, in part because elderly people are expected to attain higher incomes and therefore face fewer financial constraints," the CBO study contended. "After the turn of the century, a decline in the average number of children per family will make it less feasible for the elderly to live with their younger relatives." But even if the proportion living independently remains unchanged, the anticipated growth in the elderly population "virtually guarantees a doubling of the number of elderly people who live alone or only with their spouses by 2030."

Although most of the elderly who live alone or only with their spouses find independent living to be a good thing, for the poor or disabled it can be a significant hardship. Nevertheless, solitary residence is even fairly common among the disabled, according to the CBO study. More than two-fifths of the unmarried elderly barred from major activity by a chronic condition live alone.

As a result of the trend toward independent living, the CBO believes there may well be a demand for more assistance to the poor or disabled elderly living alone. That assistance could take the form of raising their incomes or of providing home-care services. "More broadly, a shift toward independent living among the elderly could make even those with good health and moderate incomes more dependent on formal health care and service programs that are at least partially funded by the federal government," the CBO study said.

Not everyone agrees with CBO's analysis, however. Robert H. Binstock, a professor of aging, health, and society at the Case Western Reserve University School of Medicine, in Cleveland, Ohio, pointed out that many people living independently who become chronically sick or disabled may be able to alter their living arrangements and move in with relatives or friends, or into assisted-living projects.

Concerns of the Elderly

When the twentieth century began, the elderly did not occupy a large place in American life. Only one in twenty-five people was aged sixty-five or older, and the population's median age was twenty-three. But the elderly were not isolated from the rest of society. The concept of retirement did not exist. More than two-thirds of the men sixty-five and over worked. And the elderly commonly lived with their families.

By the late 1930s, when Social Security was established, the elderly's share of the population had risen: One in fifteen people was sixty-five or older. But most elderly men "were still in the labor force, though many were unemployed," Crystal noted. "And most still depended on their jobs, savings, and families." As a result, "the initial cost of the emerging system of public benefits was remarkably low."

In the 1960s and 1970s, programs to assist the aged mushroomed. As a result, according to Crystal, there was "a revolution of rising expectations among the elderly and those approaching old age, and also among those who might once have felt individually responsible for their support." Retirement without dependency was possible. Work was no longer necessary. Today, the overwhelming majority of those over age sixty-five—84 percent of men and 93 percent of women—are not working.

Government benefits to the aged now account for more than one-fourth of the federal budget. And issues affecting the elderly now occupy the political center stage. Helping keep them there is the fact that the elderly are not only numerous, but also politically active. Their voter participation rate is high (67.7 percent reported voting in the 1984 election), and they are well organized (the American Association of Retired Persons has twenty-eight million members). This gives them considerable political clout.

Chief among the issues of concern to the elderly at the moment is long-term care. "As they age," wrote Rivlin and Wiener, "the elderly suffer not only acute illnesses requiring care in hospitals and by physicians, but chronic disabling conditions that require long-term care either at home or in nursing homes."

Most long-term care is provided by family members or friends. Few families can afford to pay for a long stay in a nursing home; the average cost in 1988 was $23,000 a year. The costs of long-term care are not covered to any significant extent by private insurance or Medicare. So the elderly have to rely on their own resources and, when those are exhausted, on Medicaid. Although not poor when they enter a nursing home, many patients soon become so, to their chagrin. "Many beneficiaries of Medicaid financing of long-term care find their unexpected status as welfare patients demeaning," said Rivlin and Wiener.

The aging of the baby boom generation and rapidly falling mortality rates mean that the demand for long-term care is bound to increase sharply. The question is whether a better way of financing such care can be found.

Sharply different views exist as to where the responsibility for financing long-term care belongs. "Some believe that the primary responsibility for care of the elderly should fall on individuals and their families, and that the government should act only as a payer of last resort for those who are unable to provide for themselves," Rivlin and Wiener observed. "The opposite view is that the government should take the lead in ensuring comprehensive care for all older people, regardless of financial need, either by providing care directly or by compulsory social insurance. In this view, there is little or no role for the private sector." Most people, they add, would probably opt for some middle ground between these opposing views.

An important fact about long-term care is that only a minority of the elderly has large long-term care expenses. On an average day, only 4.6 percent of the elderly are in nursing homes. Only 35-50 percent of the elderly spend any time in a nursing home before they die, and over 40 percent of nursing-home admissions are for ninety days or less. "Because relatively few people face long stays that involve a large outlay of funds, long-term care lends itself to insurance and risk pooling, whereby many people contribute to a fund to cover the extraordinary expenses of the few," Rivlin and Wiener wrote.

Private insurance is widely used to protect against such potential catastrophes as auto accidents, hospitalization, and premature death, but its use against the potential catastrophe of having to pay for long-term care is still relatively rare. Only about 500,000 long-term care insurance policies are in force, according to the Health Insurance Association of America. Insurance companies "remain fearful of large financial losses," Rivlin and Wiener noted. As a result, they try to screen out applicants likely to need long-term care to minimize their risks. Premiums for long-term care insurance are relatively high.

Other private-sector approaches to the financing of long-term care also seem to hold only limited promise. Continuing-care retirement communities, which provide housing, health care, and social services to the elderly who live in them, represent one such approach. In exchange for usually steep entry and monthly fees, the communities guarantee their residents appropriate care for the rest of their lives. About 680 such communities now serve about 170,000 elderly residents, according to a 1987 survey by the American Association of Homes for the Aging.

However, continuing-care retirement communities have their limitations. Most of them are geared to the affluent, requiring substantial out-of-pocket payments for use of long-term care services in addition to the regular fees. Most of them have health requirements or long waiting lists that tend to exclude from admission those elderly most likely to need long-term care, Rivlin and Wiener pointed out. Some communities have gone bankrupt, and communities with the most extensive long-term care services tend to be in the worst financial shape. Finally, most elderly people do not want to move into continuing-care retirement communities, anyway. They want to stay in their own homes.

Private-sector approaches to the long-term care problem, Rivlin and Wiener concluded, "are unlikely to be affordable by a majority of the elderly, to finance more than a modest proportion of total nursing home and home care expenditures, or to have more than a small effect on Medicaid expenditures and the number of people who spend down to Medicaid financial eligibility levels." Contending that private-sector approaches cannot supplant public spending, they urge that long-term care be covered under a general social insurance program like Medicare. "Everyone should contribute to public long-term care insurance and earn the right to needed benefits without having to prove impoverishment."

The long-term care issue is clearly not going to go away anytime soon. But that is not just because of the elderly's political influence. It is also because of the growing need.

Aged Baby Boomers

The elderly population in the United States will continue to grow, steadily but undramatically, through the first decade of the twenty-first century. But then, in 2011, when the baby boomers (those Americans born between 1946 and 1964) begin to reach age sixty-five, the growth will become dramatic indeed. There will be what Cynthia Taeuber of the Census Bureau has called a "grandparent boom." By 2020—assuming continued low birthrates, further declines in death rates, and little impact from immigration—about 17 percent of the total U.S. population will be elderly, which is almost the 1988 proportion of elderly in Florida. By 2030, according to Census Bureau projections, at least one in five Americans will be sixty-five or older. The next year, the baby boomers will start to reach age eighty-five, and the "great-grandma boom" will begin.

The changes in the coming decades "will be enormous, much more enormous than for the first three-quarters of this century," said Robert Binstock, "because I think a great many of our institutions will change. Our conception of the life course, how long it is, clearly will change. . . . In fact, I doubt if we'll be counting people as 'elderly' at the age of 65 by the year 2020."

The "elderly" baby boomers themselves are likely to be quite different from the elderly today. Because so many baby boom women are working outside the home, "more of them are more likely to have retirement and private pensions in their own name, which could make quite a difference in their economic status," Taeuber said. In addition, because the life expectancy of men is improving, the women may have their husbands around longer, and with them, their economic support.

The baby boom elderly also will be better educated than today's elderly, and since there is an apparent correlation between education and health, it's possible they will be healthier. And they may need to be. "Baby boom women have had fewer children, so there's fewer people on whom they can depend when they reach their 80s," Taeuber said.

As the four-generation family becomes commonplace in the next century, she said, "oldsters—especially women—will face the concern and expense of caring for their very old parents—and both generations will be receiving retirement benefits. For more adult workers, the care of very old, frail parents will become a problem to be faced. . . . [E]mployers should not be surprised when more workers begin requesting time off to attend to the needs of their parents. Older workers, especially women, may consider early retirement to meet the needs for care of their very old parents."

The proportion of institutionalized elderly may well grow in the coming decades, as a result of the rapid growth of the very old population, which is more subject to chronic disease. Taeuber noted that middle-aged women "have been the major source of family support for the very old but, more and more, they are in the labor force, preparing for their own old age, and hence are not as available for this task as earlier." On the other hand, medical advances may reduce the need for institutionalization.

The elderly, in general, are likely to be less isolated from the rest of society, as the concepts of "old age" and "retirement" are redefined. "Our existing policies on aging tend to isolate the aged from participating in the central institutions of our society, including the family and the workplace," Stephen Crystal wrote. "Rather than use their skills, we tend to 'pension them off' from productive social roles, or literally remove them from society by placing them, at great cost, in institutions." Lydia Bronte agreed. "I think that's something we really need to change," she said. "I think it will change anyway, because as we get larger and larger numbers of people who are over 60 and very active and very energetic and skilled and experienced, I think that those people will start changing the situation willy-nilly. But I think it would be a lot better if we all did some collective thinking about it."

The "isolation" of the elderly from the rest of society, in Bronte's view, is partly a result of "unanticipated longevity," but also is "an unanticipated consequence of something that was essentially a good step to take, that is, to provide enough money so that people could at least survive financially in their older years." The concept of retirement needs to be revised, "without pulling away the financial underpinnings of the system that we've already set up, which works very well. Social Security was an enormous step forward for this society."

Social Security, the principal source of income for the elderly, began to experience financial problems in the mid-1970s because of soaring inflation and high unemployment. Benefit obligations increased, and revenue from payroll taxes was less than expected. The situation worsened in the late 1970s and early 1980s. In addition to short-term problems, there was fear that after baby boomers started to collect benefits in the twenty-first century, the strain on the shrunken work force and on the Social Security system would become intolerable.

However, in 1983, Congress, acting on the recommendations of a bipartisan presidential commission, moved to eliminate the projected deficits of the next century. It raised the normal retirement age—the age when workers can retire and receive unreduced benefits—from sixty-five to sixty-seven, with the change to be phased in gradually starting in 2003. It delayed retirees' annual cost-of-living adjustments six months, increased payroll taxes for both employers and employees, and brought new federal employees and workers in the nonprofit sector into the system.

"The most important change, however, was to impose for the first time federal income taxes on up to half of Social Security benefits for beneficiaries with income over a specified level," wrote economist Schulz. Although this provision initially affected relatively few elderly persons, it eventually will apply to a significant number, as real and inflation-induced income increases push more and more people's "adjusted gross income," together with 50 percent of Social Security benefits, above the specified level of $25,000 (for an individual) or $32,000 (for a married couple). And those tax revenues will go into the Social Security system.

In fact, the deficits of the 1975-1982 period already have given way to surpluses, and these are expected to increase significantly in the future. "But unlike the modest surpluses of the past, legislated payroll tax levels and demographics are projected to send future surpluses in the OASDI [Old-Age, Survivors and Disability Insurance] trust funds skyrocketing," Schulz wrote. It is estimated that reserves will grow by the year 2022 to about $2.5 trillion in 1987 dollars, and then they will decline very rapidly as the baby boom generation retires. Further increases in payroll taxes may be needed after 2050.

Although "unforeseen circumstances and constantly changing economic, political, and demographic considerations make it impossible to plan Social Security's financing future with complete certainty," there now seems little cause for alarm, Schulz noted. Many baby boomers, however, still seem worried.

"I think the baby boomers are just scared," said Bell. "They're not persuaded, they just can't see how when they get to 65, the money will be there. But it will be there. If the country is here, then the money will be there. There's no question about that. But they don't quite accept that." They see "the rising [living] standard of older people and allege that therefore older people don't really need Social Security," and they "begin to look toward their own retirement." They see "the culprit which threatens their own security in old age" as "the voracious older people who are eating up all the dollars that [the baby boomers are] contributing toward support of the Social Security program." In reality, however, Bell said, the Social Security system works very well. "It's been working for 50 years, and it'll work for another 50 and more."

Fate of Children

But the future condition of Social Security is not the only worry people have about life in the aging America of the twenty-first century. There also is concern about the fate of children in such a society. "The aging society poses two possible consequences for America's children," wrote Harold A. Richman and Matthew W. Stagner of the Chapin Hall Center for Children at the University of Chicago. "They may become a treasured resource, nurtured all the more for their scarcity and importance to the nation's future, or they may come to be regarded, amid the increasing clamor for resources and attention by other dependent groups, as only another needy minority."

They find "good reason for concern" that it might be the latter, given what they regard as society's relative inattention to the needs of children in general and of poor children in particular. "Clearly, government economic support for older people has been improving, compared with support for children and their families during the early stages of the aging society," they wrote in an essay for *Our Aging Society*.

The elderly's standard of living has improved faster than that of younger people over the past three decades. And "while claiming that their own benefits are beyond challenge," Henry Fairlie wrote in the *New Republic*, "locally the old organize to oppose tax hikes to pay for school bonds." A 1983 Gallup Poll of public attitudes toward the public schools found that 45 percent of the respondents under age fifty supported an increase in taxes for public education, but only 28 percent of the respondents aged fifty and over supported it.

But many believe that the elderly's putative unconcern for the needs of children is much exaggerated, that the elderly in general are no less concerned about children than young or middle-aged people who do not have small children. "There may be some [elderly] who place their interest above all others," said Bell. "I'm sure there are. . . . But I don't think in the main that that's going to be the case. I think that the elderly are no less perfectly aware than others [of] the needs of children."

The notion, however false, that most elderly people are indifferent to the needs of children is among those notions abroad that suggest that the old stereotypes about the aged may be yielding to new ones. The elderly may now increasingly be seen as excessively well-off, greedy, politically powerful—and soon to be an intolerable burden to the rest of society.

The elderly, in Robert Binstock's view, are being made a "scapegoat," blamed for all sorts of economic and political ills. The worst instance, Binstock says, is that constantly escalating health care costs are being blamed on the elderly, with the recommended remedy being "that we don't provide life-extending [medical] care to older persons." In 1984, Richard D. Lamm, then governor of Colorado, even went so far as to suggest that elderly people "have a duty to die and get out of the way." But it is increasingly apparent that far from getting out of the way, America's elderly now, in more ways than one, represent the future.

Social Security

Passage of the Social Security Act of 1935 (PL 74-271)—one of the most comprehensive welfare bills ever cleared by Congress—was a major political event. Enacted at the urgent request of President Franklin D. Roosevelt in the midst of the worst depression in the nation's history, the act changed both the concept of personal economic security in the United States and the nature of federal-state relations in the welfare field.

A Social Revolution

The heart of the Social Security Act consisted of several "income replacement" programs. They were designed to ensure that individuals had some income for essential expenses when their regular source of income was cut off by retirement, loss of job, disability, or death of a working spouse. Of these, the main program was Old Age Insurance, a federal retirement insurance plan financed by a payroll tax, for persons presumed to be too old to work.

This was accompanied by a federal-state unemployment insurance system for persons temporarily unable to find work and a system of federal grants to the states to reimburse them for part of the costs of charity aid to the indigent—the aged, the blind, and children deprived of the support of a parent—who were unable to seek work or support themselves. Using a variety of approaches, the income replacement programs were to provide individuals with weekly or monthly cash payments from government sources to cover living expenses.

The income replacement programs represented, in many ways, a revolution in American life. Before the Roosevelt New Deal, security against old age, unemployment, and other economic hardships was considered the responsibility primarily of the individual himself, his family, and local private charitable institutions.

For isolated groups in the country—federal employees under the civil service system, some state and local government employees, and small numbers of workers covered by private pension plans at their place of employment—relatively dependable retirement pension systems did exist. But for the bulk of the population there was no systematic program—public or private—to guarantee income after retirement and no organized program at all except charity (where available) to counter economic hazards. Even the minimal level of economic security afforded the individual by these traditional and uncoordinated sources of aid often was nonexistent for much of the working population.

The Great Depression of the 1930s, which left millions destitute, generated both public pressure for some sort of economic security program and greater public willingness to accept remedial action by the federal government. Other factors leading to passage of the Social Security Act were the personal prestige of President Roosevelt and the large Democratic majorities in both houses of Congress that were ready to follow his lead.

By establishing a mandatory, nationwide program of income security, the U.S. government for the first time assumed permanent responsibility for functions traditionally reserved for the family and local governments. The income replacement programs, particularly unemployment insurance, also had the secondary function of stabilizing the national economy by keeping steady the purchasing power of different groups in good and bad economic times.

The programs furnishing income to the aged had another function that was important in the context of the depression: They were intended to help clear the labor market of the surplus of older workers competing with younger persons for scarce jobs. The expansion of benefits in ensuing years was successful in drawing eligible retirees from the work force. In other ways, however, Congress backed away from this strategy as early as 1939 when it allowed workers over sixty-five to earn up to a specified amount while continuing to receive benefits.

Insurance and Assistance

From the inception of the Social Security system, there was considerable disagreement about how the program would be financed and benefits distributed. A major issue was whether the government should use a welfare approach, an insurance approach, or both, to safeguard the individual

against economic misfortunes. In drafting the Social Security legislation in 1935, Congress devised a program that drew partly on insurance principles and partly on traditions of social welfare.

The centerpiece of the Social Security Act, Old Age Insurance, would be a large national pension system based on social insurance principles, bearing a loose resemblance to those prevailing in the private insurance industry. As with a commercial insurance company, a prospective beneficiary would pay a "premium" in the form of a payroll tax and could expect to be compensated under specified circumstances, in this case, retirement.

Congress was attracted to the insurance approach to retirement income for several reasons. It was generally believed that a self-financing insurance-type mechanism would isolate Social Security from the kind of political and economic stresses involved in deciding annual appropriations for most government programs. In addition, many experts felt the insurance method would permit benefits at a higher level than the subsistence level, providing better security for the retired individual. By making retirement benefits automatic without consideration of need or the humiliation of a means test, it was hoped that Old Age Insurance would provide surer and truer income security than a charity approach.

However, the insurance protection envisioned under Social Security departed increasingly from private-sector insurance plans. Social Security was made compulsory at the outset, and in recent years, benefits have been paid out at a faster rate than revenue has come in through the payroll tax, depleting the funds reserved for future obligations.

Congress intended Social Security payments to be one source of supplemental income to an individual after retirement.

An individual's monthly benefits were calculated through a formula based on a

Social Security Contribution and Benefit Base, Tax Rate, and Maximum Tax Payments, 1937-1988

Date	Contribution and benefit base	Employee/employer tax rate	Employee/employer maximum annual tax payment[a]
1937-1949	$ 3,000	1.000%	$ 30.00
1950	3,000	1.500	45.00
1951-1953	3,600	1.500	54.00
1954	3,600	2.000	72.00
1955-1956	4,200	2.000	84.00
1957-1958	4,200	2.250	94.50
1959	4,800	2.500	120.00
1960-1961	4,800	3.000	144.00
1962	4,800	3.125	150.00
1963-1965	4,800	3.625	174.00
1966	6,600	4.200	277.20
1967	6,600	4.400	290.40
1968	7,800	4.400	343.20
1969	7,800	4.800	374.40
1970	7,800	4.800	374.40
1971	7,800	5.200	405.60
1972	9,000	5.200	468.00
1973	10,800	5.850	631.80
1974	13,200	5.850	772.20
1975	14,100	5.850	824.85
1976	15,300	5.850	895.05
1977	16,500	5.850	965.25
1978	17,700	6.050	1,070.85
1979	22,900	6.130	1,403.77
1980	25,900	6.130	1,587.67
1981	29,700	6.650	1,975.05
1982	32,400	6.700	2,170.80
1983	35,700	6.700	2,391.90
1984	37,800	7.000	2,646.00
1985	39,600	7.050	2,791.80
1986	42,000	7.150	3,003.00
1987	43,800	7.150	3,131.70
1988	45,000	7.510	3,379.50

Source: *Social Security Bulletin: Annual Statistical Supplement, 1987.*

[a] Figures in combined years are averages.

statistically determined average life expectancy. Initially, the formula was applied to a worker's complete earnings record to yield the proper amount of the monthly payment. A retiree's Social Security payment was intended to provide a "replacement rate"— that portion of a worker's paycheck at retirement that Social Security was intended to replace—of about 40 percent.

Private pensions and savings were expected to make up the remainder of the retiree's income.

For any one year of work, a ceiling was placed on the amount that could be counted in determining a worker's lifetime earnings. This ceiling—which defined a worker's "benefit base"—began at $3,000 for the years 1937-1939.

The Old Age Insurance system was financed through a federal payroll tax, imposed on most industrial and white-collar employees and their employers. As in the calculation of benefits, the amount of a worker's annual earnings that could be taxed was initially set at $3,000. There was no tax on earnings above that amount. Assessments on taxable earnings began in 1937 at 1 percent each for employers and employees on the first $3,000 earned, rising to 2 percent each by 1954. Since then, the tax rate has increased as benefits have grown, reaching 7.51 percent in 1988.

Social Security taxes, first collected in 1937, were placed in a special trust fund account set up in the U.S. Treasury, with the money reserved for payment of pensions to eligible persons.

Payroll taxes were loosely tied to the payment of benefits in that revenues would be drawn from the same maximum earnings base that was used to calculate benefits. This contribution and benefit base would ensure that Social Security provided strictly "supplemental" retirement income, placing an upper limit on the benefit "credit" that could be amassed by any individual or family. Congress periodically hiked the maximum earnings base as average earnings increased over the years, eventually indexing it to average national wages in 1972.

Eligibility for Social Security benefits was to be a matter of right and would not depend on need. An individual would become eligible for a monthly cash payment at age sixty-five if he had worked a specified amount of time in employment subject to the payroll tax and had thus contributed to the costs of his own pension.

Charity versus Insurance

Because Old Age Insurance trust fund operations were based on actuarial principles, requiring many years before the sys-

tem built up reserves and a large number of workers became eligible, the first monthly benefits were not scheduled to be paid out until 1942. Amendments added in 1939, however, changed the effective date to 1940.

In the interim years the main burden of providing income for the aged fell on the traditional charity approach. Congress, in the 1935 act, created a separate public assistance program for the aged, called Old Age Assistance (OAA), which provided matching grants to the states to enable them to give charity aid to the indigent elderly. Need, as determined by the states through a "means test," was the sole criterion of assistance. Payments were meant to be adequate to sustain the indigent person only at or near subsistence levels. Financing came from general revenues at the federal, state, and local levels.

President Roosevelt and members of Congress emphasized that once the Old Age Insurance system was in full operation, that program was to be the primary government method of providing supplemental income for the aged. The public assistance program was only a secondary safeguard to protect those who were ineligible for insurance benefits or those whose insurance benefits were extremely low. It was expected that eventually, as more individuals built up insured status, the number of elderly requiring public assistance charity would decline proportionately.

These expectations proved correct. In 1940, the first year of monthly retirement insurance benefits, nearly 223,000 retirees received Social Security benefits, while more than two million persons received Old Age Assistance aid. By 1964 the number of beneficiaries under the expanded Old Age, Survivors and Disability Insurance (OASDI) program had swelled to close to twenty million for an increase of nearly eighteen million. Of these, about fifteen million were age sixty-two or older; the rest were dependent children, disabled persons, and other dependents. Meanwhile, the number of persons receiving Old Age Assistance benefits in 1964 had climbed by a scant 200,000. In 1982 OASDI beneficiaries numbered thirty-six million, while recipients of public assistance, by then a federal program known as Supplemental Security Income (SSI), were only four million. Of that group, fewer than half received benefits due to old age.

Financing Concepts

To achieve the long-term financing required for the Social Security Old Age Insurance system, Congress sought initially to employ a reserve method of financing. Contributions from the payroll tax were to be paid into a fund on a regular basis according to mathematical projections of future need.

Optimistic legislators were convinced that an accumulation of reserve monies would make the Social Security system relatively impregnable to fluctuations in the economy. A reserve system would permit benefit costs to be balanced against income over several decades and payroll taxes to be imposed at a more or less level rate covering the whole period.

Moreover, it was believed that, just as the adoption of a self-financing program would circumvent periodic appropriations battles in Congress, reserve financing would eliminate political fights over the rate of the payroll tax.

However, the Old Age Insurance system as actually set up in 1935 and amended in 1939 adopted somewhat relaxed reserve requirements. Under a strict scheme of reserve financing, large reserves would have to be built up so that the retirement fund at all times would have enough cash available to pay out all current and future benefits earned by individuals on the basis of work already performed. While the system was intended to build up large reserves, there was no real attempt to accumulate reserves great enough to meet all accrued liabilities, only a sizable portion.

In subsequent amendments, Congress generally raised benefit levels and expanded the program's coverage without providing adequate additional financing. This, along with strains on the program's trust funds caused by unforeseen developments in the national economy, made Social Security more of a pay-as-you-go financing system, under which, in its most extreme form, revenues would be provided only in amounts sufficient to meet current obligations, with no allowance for future requirements. Payroll tax rates simply would be adjusted each year to bring in enough funds to pay for benefits expected to be paid out that year.

The Benefits Explosion

As established, the Old Age Insurance program provided retirement benefits for the insured worker only. Over the years, however, Congress increased benefits and made more people eligible for them. Greater emphasis was placed on ensuring an adequate retirement income to an ever-increasing proportion of the population. Even before any benefits had been paid out, Congress was already broadening Social Security coverage to include beneficiaries who had never paid into the system.

The first major amendments to the Social Security Act were voted in 1939, when Congress made important structural changes in the Old Age Insurance program, broadening its scope. The most significant change authorized monthly benefits to be paid both to the dependents of an insured retiree while he was living and drawing Social Security benefits and to his survivors after his death. As a result, the program was renamed Old Age and Survivors Insur-

Social Security Benefits and Beneficiaries, 1945-1985

| | OASDI beneficiaries (in millions) | | | | | |
	Retired workers, dependents, and survivors	Disabled workers	Total	Average monthly benefits, retired workers	Covered workers (in millions)	Covered workers per OASDI beneficiary
1945	1.3	—	1.3	$ 24	46.4	42.4
1950	3.5	—	3.5	44	48.3	16.5
1955	8.0	—	8.0	62	65.2	8.6
1960	14.1	.7	14.8	74	72.5	5.1
1965	19.1	1.7	20.9	84	80.7	4.0
1970	23.6	2.7	26.2	118	93.1	3.7
1975	27.7	4.3	32.1	207	100.2	3.2
1980	30.9	4.7	35.6	341	113.0	3.2
1985	33.1	3.9	37.0	479	121.8	3.3

Sources: *Social Security Bulletin: Annual Statistical Supplement, 1987;* OASDI trustees' 1988 annual report.

ance (OASI).

To make benefits available in 1940, instead of in the original target date of 1942, the 1939 changes adopted a system of eligibility by quarters. Since then, and subject to a number of qualifications, potential Social Security beneficiaries have had to show minimum earnings for a requisite number of quarters after 1936—six in 1940—to become fully covered.

In 1983 the minimum earnings per quarter required to become eligible were $340, down from the equivalent of $568 ($50) in 1940. However, those retiring in 1983 had to have accumulated thirty-one quarters, or just under eight years, for full coverage. The requirement for full coverage was scheduled to increase to forty quarters early in the 1990s.

The 1939 amendments also introduced the concept of basing the amount of a worker's monthly Social Security payment on the worker's average monthly wage during his entire working career. Congress directed that lifetime earnings be averaged— and in later years, indexed to inflation—to yield a worker's average indexed monthly earnings. In turn, the worker's monthly benefits would be calculated by application

of the formula to his average indexed monthly earnings.

Postwar Era

Because of the long-range method of financing and other factors, the Old Age Insurance program was just hitting its operational stride when World War II ended. Relatively few people by then had become eligible for benefits, and coverage still was confined largely to urban blue collar workers. Only about $274 million was paid out in benefits in fiscal 1945.

As it began to mature, the retirement system had an ever greater impact on society. By the late 1940s there was a rapid increase in the number of beneficiaries and a corresponding rise in benefits. Whereas in 1940 fewer than a quarter of a million people received Social Security benefits totaling close to $4.1 million, by 1950 approximately 3.5 million beneficiaries were receiving monthly payments amounting to $126.9 million.

Despite substantial increases in wages and the general standard of living, the OASI system in 1950 still operated under 1939 benefit formulas and coverage rules.

As a result, the system no longer was able to fulfill its anticipated role as the primary mechanism for providing supplemental income after retirement. That led Congress to overhaul and update the entire program in 1950.

A new payroll tax schedule and a higher taxable wage base of $3,600 per year were established to bring in more revenues. In turn, the earnings ceiling upon which initial Social Security payments would be calculated also was boosted to $3,600. To compensate for increases in the cost of living, benefit levels already established by the formula would again be increased by an average of 70 percent.

The amendment substantially eased eligibility requirements for many currently aged persons and extended the basic reach of the system beyond urban employees. The self-employed (except farmers and professionals), many agricultural and domestic service workers, and state and local government workers—about 9.2 million persons—became eligible for participation in the social insurance system.

These and later changes clearly established a benefit bias in favor of persons receiving the lowest retirement benefits. For them, increases in benefits were proportionately higher than for those persons receiving the maximum benefits.

Other changes during the 1950s continued to expand the retirement system by increasing benefits and easing eligibility requirements. In 1952 benefits were raised slightly but the increases were not substantial. In 1954, however, the taxable wage and benefit base was increased to $4,200 a year, a new, higher tax schedule was set, and benefits were increased further. Some 7.5 million more persons were brought under Social Security coverage, including self-employed farmers, additional farm and domestic workers, and additional government and nonprofit organization employees. After the 1954 amendments, about 80 percent of the paid labor force was covered by the retirement system.

In 1956, Congress made two major changes in the Social Security law. In the postwar years, the question of whether the system should assume responsibility for supporting disabled persons below retirement age was a controversial issue. A public assistance program, Aid to the Permanently and Totally Disabled, had been set up for the disabled in 1950. Congress linked that program to the Social Security system in 1956, establishing a separate Disability Insurance (DI) trust fund to provide benefits to long-term and permanently disabled workers aged fifty to sixty-four. The Social Security program was renamed Old Age, Survivors and Disability Insurance (OASDI).

The 1956 amendments also reduced the minimum benefit age for women from sixty-five to sixty-two, with actuarially reduced benefits in some cases.

Two years later benefits again were raised slightly, the taxable wage base was increased to $4,800 a year, and a new Social Security tax schedule, set at 2.5 percent, took effect in 1959. Dependents of workers receiving monthly Disability Insurance payments also were made eligible for monthly dependents benefits.

A Broadening Constituency

During the economic prosperity of the 1950s and 1960s, workers' wages increased at a relatively rapid rate compared with price increases. Between 1950 and 1972, wages increased by an average of 4.7 percent annually, while prices rose only 2.5 percent. As a result, the Social Security trust funds built up a heavy cushion of reserves from the payroll tax levied on the relatively higher earnings. Congress continued to expand benefits under Social Security, which was becoming an increasingly popular and politically appealing program for winning votes back home.

Although there were no general benefit increases in 1960, Congress did remove the minimum age of fifty for receipt of Disability Insurance benefits and loosened general eligibility requirements for Social Security benefits. In 1961 eligibility requirements were eased again, a higher schedule of tax rates replaced the one set up in 1958, and benefits were increased for some groups of workers. In addition, the minimum age at which men could receive benefits was dropped from sixty-five to sixty-two, with actuarially reduced benefits if a worker chose to retire at the earlier age instead of waiting for "full" retirement at sixty-five.

By the end of 1964, about 90 percent of all employment in the nation was covered by the expanded Old Age, Survivors and Disability Insurance program. Approximately 76 percent of the nation's aged were receiving benefits under the program, with another 8 percent eligible but not drawing benefits because they either had not yet retired or had not applied for them. The total amount paid out by the Social Security system in fiscal 1964 to approximately twenty million people was nearly $16.2 billion, compared with the $274 million paid to beneficiaries in fiscal 1945. The average monthly benefit for a retired worker had climbed from $22.60 when benefits were first distributed in 1940 to $83.92 in 1965.

In short, the Old Age, Survivors and Disability Insurance program had become the nation's single most important entitlement program by the early 1960s, accounting in fiscal 1964 for 37 percent of all welfare expenditures compared with only 6 percent in fiscal 1950.

The U.S. social insurance system carved out a yet deeper niche in the federal budget when Congress in 1965 established a major medical care program for the aged under the Social Security system. The health care issue had come up repeatedly in the postwar years. President Harry S Tru-

man had proposed a health insurance program covering a large portion of the population. President John F. Kennedy began in 1960 to press for a federally operated health insurance program for the elderly.

Legislation passed in 1965 provided a new payroll tax (applied equally to employers, employees, and the self-employed) and a taxable earnings base to finance the new Medicare program enacted that year. Federal tax revenues were expected to finance the plan for persons not covered by Social Security. The Health Insurance payroll taxes and general revenues earmarked for the plan were placed in a new Hospital Insurance (HI) trust fund, separate from the system's OASI and DI trust funds.

The 1965 law also made other significant changes in Social Security, including a 7 percent increase in retirement benefits. These were followed by new expansions of the Social Security Act during the Lyndon B. Johnson administration. Congress raised retirement benefits again in 1967, this time by 13 percent, and continued to ease Social Security eligibility requirements.

Rising inflation in the late 1960s—due in part to expanded government programs and increasing federal deficits as the Johnson administration's Great Society programs took hold—led Congress to raise OASDI benefits three times between 1969 and 1972: 15 percent in 1969, 10 percent in 1971, and 20 percent in 1972.

In addition, various eligibility requirements for the OASDI program were considerably eased. To finance the increased benefits, the amount of earnings subject to the Social Security tax was substantially increased. The taxable earnings base jumped from $4,800 in 1965 to $10,800 in 1973. Increases in the tax rate itself, which caused greater hardship for lower-income workers, were not as great, rising from 3.625 to 5.85 percent over the same period. (Part of this increase was necessary to put the Medicare trust fund on a more stable basis.)

OASDI Fund Operations, 1970-1986

Year	Income (in billions)	Outgo (in billions)	Fund increase (in billions)	Fund at year-end (in billions)	Reserve ratio at beginning of year
1970	$ 37.0	$ 33.1	$ 3.9	$38.1	103%
1971	40.9	38.5	2.4	40.4	99
1972	45.6	43.3	2.3	42.8	93
1973	54.8	53.1	1.6	44.4	80
1974	62.1	60.6	1.5	45.9	73
1975	67.6	69.2	−1.5	44.3	66
1976	75.0	78.2	−3.2	41.1	57
1977	82.0	87.3	−5.3	35.9	47
1978	91.9	96.0	−4.1	31.7	37
1979	105.9	107.3	−1.5	30.3	30
1980	119.7	123.6	−3.8	26.5	25
1981	142.5	144.4	−1.9	24.5	18
1982	147.9	160.1	.2	24.8	15
1983	171.3	171.2	.09	24.9	14
1984	186.6	180.4	6.2	31.1	17
1985	203.5	190.6	11.1	42.2	21
1986	216.8	201.5	4.7	46.9	23

Sources: *Social Security Bulletin: Annual Statistical Supplement, 1987;* Social Security Administration.

All of these benefit and tax rate changes were added piecemeal to bills dealing with other subjects. It was not until 1972 that Congress approved a comprehensive revision of the Social Security Act itself.

Social Security Overextended

In 1972, the large trust fund reserves resulting from the relative buoyancy of wage levels—and therefore of payroll tax receipts—in the 1950s and 1960s led Congress to make basic changes in the way benefit increases were calculated.

Instead of increasing benefits on an ad hoc basis, often involving intense political fights, Congress in 1972 decided to tie future increases in Social Security benefits to the Consumer Price Index (CPI). Some members maintained that benefits from Social Security still were relatively low and that a healthy economy and rising wages would generate adequate revenues to cover future increases. Conservative members— perhaps the most important advocates of indexing—saw it as a way to keep benefits down by insulating the process from the pressure of benefit-hungry constituents.

Congress provided for automatic benefit increases beginning in 1975, when the cost of living rose at an annual rate of more than 3 percent. In years of price inflation above 3 percent, both the initial benefit formula and the rate of subsequent benefit hikes would be increased accordingly. And Congress tied the wage base on which Social Security taxes were levied to a wage index that also was expected to increase.

The 1972 legislation also made a revolutionary shift in the structure of Social Security. A new program of assistance to the aged poor—Supplemental Security Income (SSI)—was set up as a replacement for the original Old Age Assistance program. Unlike the OAA, the new program was to be fully financed by the federal government from general tax revenues and would set uniform national eligibility requirements. Old Age Assistance had been a jointly funded federal-state program. The SSI program provided benefits in 1975 to more than four million persons, compared with 3.2 million under the entire federal-state public assistance program that had preceded it. In 1979 between 8 percent and 9 percent of the population age sixty-five and over received Supplemental Security Income, while approximately 90 percent received Social Security payments.

The First Deficits

These developments caused a greater intermingling of welfare policies with the insurance principle conceived in the original Social Security Act. They also precipitated a multitude of financial problems for the benefit-heavy social insurance program.

The price indexing of benefits made Social Security even more dependent on the economy's performance. Although indexing seemed logical in the context of 1950s and 1960s prosperity, the relationship between wages and prices—in which the former had outpaced the latter—changed drastically during the 1970s as the national economy took a series of sharp downturns.

The cost of rising benefits outpaced the tax increases provided by the 1972 amendments, and by the mid-1970s the first signs of Social Security's financial troubles had become apparent. After 1975 the OASI trust fund consistently paid out more to Social Security beneficiaries than it collected from payroll taxes. By relying on its reserves between 1975 and 1981, the system was able to keep delivering benefits. By 1981 the reserves had been cut into by more than $15 billion for that purpose.

In its 1977 annual report, the Social Security Board of Trustees—the secretaries of the Departments of Labor, Treasury, and Health, Education and Welfare (since 1979, Health and Human Services)—projected

that the Social Security system's Disability Insurance fund's reserves would be exhausted by 1979 and that the retirement and survivors' benefits fund would run out of money in the early 1980s. Although there were other contributing factors, the main cause of these shortfalls was the combination of prolonged inflation and recession, which caused Social Security benefit costs to rise and which reduced revenues from the payroll tax. Government actuaries and other experts predicted grave financial strains for the Social Security system.

Correcting an Error

The Carter administration in May 1977 proposed a Social Security rescue plan based on gradual increases in employer, but not employee, tax contributions into the system. The proposal also included transfers of general revenues to the dwindling trust funds to make up for revenues lost during the 1970s periods of relatively high unemployment when fewer workers were paying into the retirement system.

Carter's plan was designed to provide an additional $83 billion to the funds by 1982. The president said that his proposals would achieve that goal without raising payroll taxes for low- and middle-income workers, thus fulfilling a 1976 election campaign pledge. However, Carter's plan made little headway in Congress.

After considering some innovative financing schemes, Congress in 1977 decided to rely exclusively on traditional payroll taxes to replenish the shrinking reserves in the trust funds. The 1977 Social Security tax increase—intended to yield $227 billion in ten years—was the nation's largest peacetime tax increase ever. The measure set new, steeper tax schedules that steadily increased both the tax rate and the taxable earnings base for both employee and employer equally, from 1979 through 1990.

Taxed at the maximum rate, a worker's

Social Security taxes would more than triple by 1987. In 1977, with payroll taxes set at 5.85 percent each for employer and employee on a worker's earnings up to $16,500, the maximum Social Security tax paid by a worker and his employer was $965 each. In 1987, when the tax rate was set to rise to 7.15 percent on a projected earnings base of up to $42,900, each could expect to pay more than $3,000 a year into the Social Security system.

The 1977 Social Security changes also took a modest step toward reducing Social Security expenditures by including an important administration-backed measure to correct a technical flaw in the formula for computing the starting benefit levels of future retirees.

The 1972 amendments had permitted increases in both wage levels and prices to influence the formulas for calculating the initial benefits of new retirees. This meant that when the Consumer Price Index rose, it affected overall benefit levels in two ways: by increasing certain factors in the formula for calculating initial benefits and by boosting the annual amount of subsequent benefit hikes. Depending on the performance of the economy, the resulting overcompensation for inflation could have allowed recipients' benefits to exceed their preretirement wages and threatened to send benefits skyrocketing over the next several decades.

To correct the problem, Congress in 1977 separated ("decoupled") the process of granting annual cost-of-living Social Security increases to already retired persons from the computation of their initial benefit levels. Under the 1977 law, the formula used for intitial benefits would be affected only by changes in the average level of wages, not prices.

Further Belt Tightening

The 1977 law also eased the earnings test, allowing elderly persons to earn more money without losing a portion of their benefits, and liberalized the treatment of divorced and widowed beneficiaries. The Carter administration had criticized those changes as too costly.

It soon became evident that the 1977 amendments would not restore the system to financial health. Carter in 1979 urged Congress to eliminate a number of "unnecessary" Social Security benefits.

That Carter would even mention the possibility of reducing benefits reflected a major shift in thinking about Social Security, since Congress historically had done little but increase benefits. Among the changes Carter proposed were a phase-out of education benefits for dependent children age eighteen and over, a cut-off in surviving parent benefits after the youngest child had reached age sixteen, and elimination of the minimum benefit guarantee.

Acknowledging that the system was becoming too expensive, Congress in May 1980 attempted to roll back Social Security payments slightly by reducing Disability Insurance benefits to workers who became disabled after July 1 of that year. Provisions of the 1980 law were expected to reduce Social Security and welfare spending by $2.6 billion in fiscal 1981 through 1985.

Later in 1980, Congress opted for a politically appealing "stopgap" solution to the system's impending financial crisis. Under election-year pressures, members agreed to reallocate funds from the Disability Insurance fund to the OASI fund in 1980-1981 to ensure that there would be sufficient revenue to pay beneficiaries. However, by this action, Congress merely postponed the financial crisis for a few more years.

Partisan Deadlocks

In the first year of the Reagan administration, talk of lopping off benefits and adopting cost-cutting policies intensified.

However, Social Security had developed a vast constituency over the years, and any efforts to change the system—particularly cuts in benefits—had become highly politicized. The funding crisis required urgent action, but the partisan labels that accompanied suggested changes in Social Security caused the president and Congress to abandon comprehensive reforms in 1981.

Outlining his program for economic recovery in February 1981, President Reagan proposed short- and long-term approaches to Social Security's problems.

The main component of Reagan's short-term strategy was a proposal to eliminate as of July 1981 the minimum benefit program, which provided a payment of $122 a month to anyone eligible for Social Security, regardless of the person's employment and wage history. The administration sought particularly to cut off the windfall available to certain beneficiaries—often retired government workers with generous federal pensions—who worked only a short time in employment covered by Social Security. (Federal civil service workers were not covered by Social Security.) While the House and the Senate went along with this plan in their 1981 budget bills, both houses reversed themselves later that year, voting to restore the minimum monthly benefit.

Meanwhile, President Reagan set off a firestorm of controversy by proposing drastic changes in the Social Security system to protect it from financial insolvency. His plan included a reduction in benefits for early retirement at age sixty-two, a one-time three-month delay in the annual cost-of-living allowance (COLA), tougher eligibility requirements for disability payments, and an altered benefit formula that would have reduced initial benefits for future retirees.

Reaction on Capitol Hill and across the nation ranged from skepticism to outright anger. Congressional critics including House Speaker Thomas P. O'Neill, Jr., D-

Mass., House Select Aging Committee chairman Claude Pepper, D-Fla., and Sen. Daniel Patrick Moynihan, D-N.Y., charged the plan was unnecessary. They saw it as a backdoor attempt to reduce the federal budget deficit. Not surprisingly, groups representing the elderly immediately voiced their opposition to the Reagan package and predicted a major outcry when the American people became aware of what the impact of the proposals would be.

Acknowledging the political sensitivity of the issue, Reagan backpedaled on his reform plan within a week of its announcement. Administration officials insisted that almost everything in the proposals was negotiable. Against this backdrop, congressional leaders on the Social Security issue—Senate Finance Committee chairman Robert Dole, R-Kan., Sen. William Armstrong, R-Colo., and Rep. J. J. Pickle, D-Texas—sought to accommodate the president to some degree in the belief that bipartisan support would be necessary to push comprehensive Social Security reforms through Congress.

But the issue had become so politicized during the year that major changes were not feasible. Dole's committee was unable to reach agreement on a comprehensive reorganization package and instead approved a short-term funding solution to tide the system over through the mid-1980s. The final legislation, approved by Congress in December 1981, restored the minimum benefit payment for those already eligible, but eliminated it for those retiring after December 31, 1981. The bill also allowed the financially troubled Old Age and Survivors Insurance trust fund to borrow from the somewhat healthier disability and hospital insurance trust funds through the end of 1982.

Perhaps the most important development of 1981 was Reagan's request that Congress form a bipartisan task force to address long-term funding problems. Congress complied, and Reagan asked the commission to submit a report by December 31, 1982, after the midterm congressional elections.

Greenspan Commission

The National Commission on Social Security Reform proved to be the right vehicle for getting comprehensive Social Security reforms through Congress. The commission consisted of five members appointed by the House Speaker, five appointed by the Senate majority leader, and five by the president. Eight of the fifteen members were Republicans and seven were Democrats.

A conscious effort was made by Chairman Alan Greenspan (chairman of the Council of Economic Advisers under Richard Nixon) to avoid controversy until after the November 1982 elections. Thus, for most of 1982, the volatile Social Security issue was buried in the commission's private meetings. The panel reserved all decision making until a three-day brainstorming session that was held November 11-13.

After a somewhat faltering start during its November meetings, the commission in January 1983 approved a set of recommendations that paved the way for quick congressional action to keep the retirement system afloat for the rest of the century. The compromise was most specific on the question of raising revenues, recommending that the system raise $168 billion for calendar years 1983-1989. This would be accomplished by a variety of controversial and innovative mechanisms, including a six month COLA delay, a higher payroll tax schedule, the inclusion of federal employees under Social Security, and the taxation of a certain percentage of benefits.

The commission was divided on how to solve a projected Social Security shortfall in the twenty-first century when the baby boom generation would begin to retire and there would be insufficient workers paying into the fund. Generally, Republicans favored increasing the retirement age while Democrats preferred to increase the payroll tax even further.

The widespread endorsement of the commission package gave members a relatively easy way to take the necessary, but politically difficult, steps for keeping the system from going broke.

In March 1983, Congress finally approved a massive overhaul of Social Security (PL 98-21), ending almost two years of partisan wrangling and congressional stalemate. Congress was able to resolve the long-term funding dispute after accepting Republican demands that the retirement age be pushed back from sixty-five to sixty-seven by the year 2027 (to sixty-six by 2009, to sixty-seven by 2027). Otherwise, the basic parameters of the Social Security revisions largely conformed to the January recommendations of the Greenspan commission. Key provisions of the legislation delayed the annual COLA six months—beginning in 1984, COLA payments would be made in January, not July, of each year—and increased payroll taxes periodically throughout the 1980s for both employees and employers.

Congress also made a fundamental change in the Social Security concept by taxing benefits of high-income recipients and by using transfers from the general Treasury to help bolster the system's trust funds. It also voted to bring new federal employees, members of Congress, the president, the vice president, and federal judges under the Social Security system.

Financing Problem

When it passed the 1977 amendments, Congress thought it had settled the Social Security financing problem. But the system's money troubles apparently had only just begun. Unforeseen economic difficulties—double-digit inflation, economic recession and stagnation, low productivity, and sustained high unemployment—reduced the revenues needed to replenish the Social Security trust funds.

Even with the steep increases in the tax rate and the wage indexation of the taxable earnings base set up in the 1977 amendments, revenues expected from the payroll tax dropped as a result of high unemployment in the late 1970s and the long-term trend toward early retirement. Meanwhile, payments to beneficiaries rose unexpectedly due to inflation.

Congress's 1972 decision to index Social Security benefit payments to the CPI (starting in 1975) turned out to be much more costly than anticipated. In 1975 the indexing formula gave retirees a 14.3 percent cost-of-living increase in benefits. And while the 1977 changes corrected the gross excesses in the calculation of initial benefits that had occurred in 1972, they left the indexation of subsequent benefits intact.

Cost-of-living increases after 1977 continued to outstrip the projections of the OASDI trustees—reaching 14 percent instead of an anticipated 5 percent in 1980 and 11 percent instead of 4 percent in 1981. They increased 7.5 percent in July 1982.

Perhaps the greatest short-term damage was wrought by the relationship between wages and prices caused by inflation. The indexation of benefits to prices would serve the system well as long as wages rose as fast or faster than prices, and, correspondingly, as long as payroll tax revenues exceeded the cost of Social Security payments. Wages had grown faster than prices for more than twenty years before 1972, and Congress assumed that they would continue to do so. While the 1977 amendments made some adjustments for the magnitude of benefits being paid out after 1972, they did not alter the funda-

mental economic assumptions upon which the indexation scheme was based. When the relationship between wages and prices was reversed after 1977, the system's trust funds suddenly were burdened with unanticipated strains.

Unemployment also cost the system revenues. For every one million workers who were laid off for a single month in 1980, approximately $100 million in anticipated employee and employer taxes to the Social Security trust funds were lost. Most experts agreed that heavy unemployment, on top of high inflation, could also act as an impetus for an increasing number of workers to retire earlier than actuaries originally projected, thus reducing anticipated Social Security revenues and increasing benefit payments sooner than expected. As retirees seemed to be better protected against rampant inflation than workers paying into the system, it not surprising that there was an increase in the number of persons retiring before age sixty-five.

Other social and economic trends—including low birth and mortality rates, increased participation of women in the work force, and the slow rate of economic growth—also contributed to the financial strains burdening the Social Security system.

When the Greenspan commission submitted its report in January 1983, the Social Security system's Old Age and Survivors Insurance trust fund was on the brink of insolvency. The interfund borrowing authority granted by Congress in 1981 had expired in December 1982, and, as the conference report had specified, would ensure "benefit payments for a period [no] more than six months beyond the date of such determination." If Congress had not honored the commission's recommendations later that year and passed a new Social Security law, the OASI trust fund would have run short of funds in June 1983 and benefit payments would have ceased.

The new law was also intended to meet a large discrepancy between expenditures and revenues that threatened to plague the funds for the rest of the decade. Even if Congress had allowed OASI to continue relying on loans from the system's two other funds, all three likely would have run out of money sometime in 1984. If this happened, not only would the retirement fund have dried up, but Medicare and disability payments—financed by the system's other trust funds—would have stopped as well.

A Long-term Problem

Even if the economy could be stabilized and Social Security costs contained through the end of the twentieth century, a much more serious crisis looms in the long run for the retirement income system. The basic problem is that, by about the year 2020, significantly fewer workers will be supporting more retirees, which eventually could result in considerably higher Social Security costs per worker.

While unexpected economic developments caused the short-term cash-flow problems of the system, unforeseen demographic trends have altered the statistical basis on which the system was founded and promise to plague Social Security in the future. The growing percentage of the U.S. population over sixty-five has skewed the population as a whole so that the number of workers paying into the Social Security system has been shrinking in relation to the number of individuals receiving benefits since the system was first set up. The strain has been compounded by the fact that, with increased longevity, more benefits are paid over the lifetime of each retiree. Following what is likely to be a slack period between 1990 and 2020, the demographic imbalances resulting from the post-World War II baby boom, plus a decline in the national birth rate, will join with these factors, threatening to put nearly intolerable bur-

dens on pension systems—both public and private—by the early twenty-first century.

The Demographic Factors

As Peter G. Peterson, a commerce secretary in the Nixon administration, observed in March 1983, "demographics will hold very few surprises since almost every new worker by the year 2000 has already been born and can be counted." Thus the number of retirees in the next century also can easily be determined. Policy makers know pretty well what to expect in terms of Social Security benefit payments. It remains to be seen, however, how other factors, such as the fertility rate and immigration, will affect the size of the contributing population of 2020.

More Retirees/Fewer Workers

At the beginning of the twentieth century, only 4 percent of the U.S. population lived beyond age sixty-five; the average life expectancy was forty-nine years. By the mid-1980s the percentage had tripled; and life expectancy was seventy-one years for males and seventy-eight years for females.

According to a May 1981 Census Bureau report, there were 25.5 million Americans over age sixty-five in 1980—a 28 percent increase over 1970. In 1987 nearly 30 million people in the United States were over age sixty-five—about 12 percent of the total population.

These numbers were expected to grow steadily through the end of the century. By the year 2020, when the postwar baby-boom generation is retiring, Dr. Beth J. Soldo of the Center for Population Research in Washington, D.C., calculated that there would be 45 million persons over age sixty-five—16 percent of an expected U.S. population of 290 million.

In addition to the greater longevity of the present U.S. population, there has been a sharp decline in the birthrate. Consequently the median age of the population has been increasing steadily. It was twenty-nine years in 1940 when the Social Security program was gearing up and reached thirty years in 1980. By the century's end it is expected to climb to thirty-six. In subsequent decades, as the postwar generation reaches retirement age, the median age is expected to pass age thirty-eight.

Steadily decreasing birthrates resulted in the so-called "baby bust" of the 1970s and early 1980s. Contributing factors included improved methods and increased use of contraceptives and postponement of child-bearing until women reach their late twenties or thirties. Moreover, a larger percentage of couples wanted only one or two children compared with parents of earlier generations.

The birthrate at the height of the postwar baby boom in 1957 was 25.3 births per one thousand persons; by 1976 it had fallen to 14.8, only four points above the all-time low during the 1930s Great Depression. While there have been some indications of an increase in fertility trends recently—the birthrate was 16.2 in 1980—there is no evidence of a future explosion in birth rates above the current low trends.

The Dependency Ratio

Barring unforeseen developments in U.S immigration policy and other demographic trends, the plummeting birthrate means there will be far fewer numbers of young people entering the work force. Decreasing numbers of active workers will have to support a much enlarged retired population in the years ahead.

Whereas more than one hundred workers were paying into the Social Security system to support each retiree when the program was getting started in the early 1940s, the ratio of contributors to beneficiaries had dropped to about three workers for each retiree in 1980. This "dependency ratio"—the number of workers paying into the Social Security system in proportion to the number of retirees and dependents receiving benefits out of the trust funds—was expected to decrease steadily through the middle of the twenty-first century. Soon after the baby-boom generation, born in 1945 through 1959, retires, the dependency ratio is expected to drop dramatically, to approximately two workers supporting each retiree.

Early Retirement/Longevity

This gloomy forecast is complicated by two other factors. First, more and more American workers have been opting for early retirement. In 1977 about 77 percent of the recently retired men and 79 percent of the recently retired women took reduced early retirement Social Security benefits, available before age sixty-five. Although some evidence suggests the trend might be changing in the face of continued inflationary pressures, the early retirement factor has accelerated the decline in the Social Security trust funds.

Second, medical advances, better nutrition, and other changes in lifestyles have resulted, as noted earlier, in greater longevity. Americans are living in retirement longer than in the past. When Social Security was enacted in 1935, the average person who retired at age sixty-five spent 12.8 years in retirement. According to the February 1981 final report of the President's Commission on Pension Policy, that statistic had jumped to sixteen years and presumably would continue growing. The 1982 OASDI trustees' annual report projected an average life expectancy for sixty-five-year-old men and women in the year 2020 of 19.8 years.

Assessing the Problem

An article published in 1982 by the Federal Reserve Bank of New York observed that the "basic problem is that . . .

average retirees both now and in the future can expect to receive benefits that, by any measure, are far in excess of lifetime contributions.... The difficulties of Social Security are almost entirely the result of the fact that a self-financed system cannot continue to pay out subsidies forever."

What makes the situation especially alarming is that today's workers have been forced to subsidize today's retirees at rather high rates *and* at the same time build up reserves for their own retirement. This is because the dependency ratio is expected to further deteriorate when the baby-boom generation retires.

Whether the burden is bearable or not will depend on a number of long-range factors that cannot be predicted with any great certainty. These include the evolution of political attitudes toward Social Security, economic growth rates, and demographic trends. Demographic trends, in particular, are volatile, and many developments in the U.S. population—the baby boom, for example—were not predicted by professional demographers.

If fertility rates rise more sharply than expected in the next two decades, then the burden of supporting the baby-boom generation in retirement could be lighter than currently anticipated. However, fertility rates also could turn out to be even lower than expected, and in that case the problems facing the system after the year 2020 will be even more serious than the pessimists now predict.

Another unknown factor is the role immigrants will play in the coming decades. Since immigrants tend to be younger than the population as a whole, many of them could still be in the work force when the baby-boom generation retires. Moreover, illegal immigrants may never claim the benefits for which they have contributed via the payroll tax, either because they are afraid to disclose their identities to authorities or because they have left the country.

In a 1983 *New York Review of Books* article, Alicia Munnell was optimistic about the long-term future. She projected a larger and wealthier tax-paying generation—resulting from a higher fertility rate and high rates of legal and illegal immigration—that she thought could bear the burden of future benefits. Peterson, on the other hand, predicted that if the system went unchanged, workers in the next century could be paying 44 percent of their paychecks to the Social Security system.

In any event, as one expert pointed out, as long as Social Security is "financed by intergenerational transfers instead of by the contributions of the recipients themselves, the system will be vulnerable to demographic shifts that legislation cannot fully anticipate."

Lane Kirkland, president of the AFL-CIO and member of the Greenspan commission, however, warned in 1982 against characterizing the Social Security crunch as an intergenerational dispute. Young people benefit from survivor and disability payments, he pointed out, and they live more happily in the knowledge that their parents will be provided for. Others have made the argument that short- and long-term problems should not be lumped together. They saw little point in worrying about future problems in the system when immediate problems demanded resolution.

Courting Public Opinion

Other than the funding exigencies of the Social Security system, the American public's lack of confidence in its soundness has been a factor in provoking remedial action on behalf of the retirement funds. In an April 1981 survey conducted for the National Federation of Independent Business, 68 percent of those persons interviewed said they felt the Social Security program was in trouble financially; only 18 percent expressed confidence that the system was financially sound.

A May 1980 nationwide poll ordered by the National Commission on Social Security found that most U.S. workers under the age of fifty-five feared that the system would not have enough money to pay their benefits when they retired. A staggering 73 percent of those interviewed between the ages of twenty-five and forty-four expressed little or no confidence in the system's ability to pay future benefits. Of persons aged forty-five to fifty-four, 56 percent lacked confidence in the system. On the other hand, 58 percent of those between the ages of fifty-five and sixty-four—and 74 percent of the elderly—had a great deal of faith in it.

In a similar survey conducted by CBS News and the *New York Times* in mid-1981, after President Reagan had announced his proposed cutbacks in the program, approximately 73 percent of workers age eighteen to twenty-nine felt the retirement income system would not have sufficient funds to pay their benefits. In the thirty- to forty-four-year-old age group, 67 percent said the Social Security system would not be able to pay their benefits. About 40 percent of those age forty-five to fifty-four felt the same way. In marked contrast to the 1980 survey, only 54 percent of persons over age sixty-five showed confidence in the Social Security system; 13 percent indicated the system would not be able to pay their benefits and 33 percent expressed no opinion.

Any talk of radically restructuring Social Security touched raw nerves, as Republicans found out in the 1982 congressional elections. The week before the November election, the National Republican Congressional Committee found it advisable to withdraw a fund-raising letter in which contributors to the party were asked to choose between different options for reforming the Social Security system, among them a proposal to make the system voluntary.

With the failure of Congress to rectify Social Security's finances in the late 1970s and early 1980s in mind, many experts argued that Congress needed to address the "fundamental" problems confronting the system and not just "tinker around the edges."

Drawing on work done in the early 1970s by Martin Feldstein, chairman of the Council of Economic Advisers under Reagan, and A. Haeworth Robertson, chief actuary of the Social Security Administration from 1935 to 1978, Peterson argued that the growing burden of Social Security taxation was retarding the country's rate of investment and economic growth. Comparing the United States with Japan, where rates of investment in new plant and equipment, public infrastructure, and civilian research and development have been much higher, Peterson attributed the difference partly to the fact that "pensions in Japan—both public and private—are meager, forcing workers to save for their retirement."

Not all economists have agreed with this line of reasoning, however. In a book published in November 1982, Henry Aaron, a senior fellow at the Brookings Institution, a think tank in Washington, D.C., asserted that the evidence was inconclusive as to whether Social Security has had significant detrimental effects on the level of U.S. savings and labor supply. On the other hand, Aaron cited strong evidence that Social Security had greatly improved the economic status of the aged. Aaron found that Social Security provided 39 percent of the total money income of the elderly in 1978 and 76 percent of the income of the elderly poor.

Under pressure by the public and in a highly partisan atmosphere, members of the Greenspan commission in 1982-1983 sought a realistic compromise solution that would transcend the failed remedies of the past. Chairman Alan Greenspan pushed for the use of realistic economic assumptions in the commission's deliberations to prevent further erosion of public confidence.

Rescuing Social Security

There has been no shortage of official reports and studies on why the Social Security program was experiencing money troubles and how they could be solved. In December 1979 the Advisory Council on Social Security—which was required by law to report every four years on the status of the Social Security system—supplied Congress with a long list of proposals for strengthening the system. In 1981 numerous study panels, including president-elect Ronald Reagan's Social Security Task Force, the President's Commission on Pension Policy, and the National Commission on Social Security Reform, all offered alternatives for making the retirement income system financially sound.

Many of these proposals for basic changes in the Social Security system, such as funding some benefit payments through general tax revenues, had been recommended to Congress as early as 1938. Although Congress over the years put many recommendations into law, significant changes failed to win approval.

Three basic alternatives had been suggested: raising payroll taxes steeply, reducing benefits substantially, or letting the federal deficit increase. But any of these adjustments in such a massive and popular program as Social Security would be painful ones—both politically and economically—and would affect virtually every citizen in one way or another. Increased taxes or large federal deficits would hinder economic growth; cuts in benefits could devastate elderly persons who relied on Social Security as their sole source of retirement income. When difficult choices were made, as in 1977 when substantial tax increases

were approved, their effects were negated by the institutional bias toward increasing benefits that became entrenched during times of economic prosperity and program growth.

Each time a Social Security crisis arose after 1977, Congress responded with a "band-aid" solution, juggling funds from one trust fund to another. Many members recognized that while they may have been saving the day by these transfers, they were courting disaster in the long run.

By contrast, the January 1983 recommendations of the bipartisan National Commission on Social Security Reform were unprecedented in their comprehensive treatment of Social Security issues. Just as the commission provided a badly needed vehicle for compromise among divergent political views, its suggested reforms attempted to apportion the heavy burden of resuscitating the system evenly among the presently employed and current beneficiaries, the rich and poor, and later generations of participants in the system.

Of the prospective remedies for the funding crisis, those raising revenue were the most numerous. Policy makers, fearful of the political repercussions of cutting Social Security benefits, searched for new sources of revenue for the troubled social insurance system. This spawned a wide variety of schemes.

Payroll Tax Hike

Although raising the paryroll tax presented a politically distasteful move, some Social Security experts had recommended an even higher rate than those increases that had been scheduled under the 1977 amendments. The April 1981 final report of the National Commission on Social Security recommended changing the tax rate schedule so that the trust funds would be adequately financed with a contingency reserve of at least one year's benefit payments

Major Provisions of . . .

Following are the major provisions of the Social Security rescue plan signed into law April 20, 1983 (PL 98-21).

Enhanced Tax Revenues

● Increase employer and employee payroll taxes. Would be .3 percent less for employees than for employers in 1984. Difference to be made up by income tax credit.
● Increase payroll taxes for self-employed individuals by 33 percent to equal the combined tax paid by employers and employees.
● Tax as regular income the Social Security benefits of individuals with adjusted gross income over $25,000; $32,000 for a married couple filing a joint return.

COLA Cuts, Adjustments

● Delay the July 1983 cost-of-living allowance six months.
● Adjust the annual COLA indexation to lesser of wages and prices whenever Old Age and Survivors Insurance (OASI) or Disability Insurance (DI) reserve ratios fall below 15 percent (20 percent after 1988).

Increasing Retirement Age

● Gradually increase the retirement age from sixty-five to sixty-seven by 2027.
● Liberalize the penalty currently placed on retirees with outside earnings.
● Increase the benefit bonus individuals receive for delaying retirement.
● Require the secretary of health and human services to study the effects of the retirement age change on those who are forced to retire early because of physically demanding work.

Accounting

● Require the Treasury to credit the Social Security trust funds at the beginning of each month with all payroll taxes expected that month.
● Allow the three Social Security trust funds—OASI, DI, and Hospital Insurance (HI)—to borrow funds from each other through 1987.
● Permanently reallocate payroll taxes from the DI trust fund to the OASI trust fund.
● Remove the Social Security system from the "unified" federal budget, beginning in fiscal year 1992.

(a reserve ratio of 100 percent). Others suggested changing the Social Security law so that a covered employee's income exempt from the payroll tax—interest, rents, profits, or other unearned income—would be subject to Social Security taxes, thus generating additional revenues.

However, additional taxes were not considered a real policy option in 1981 because members of Congress feared they

... the 1983 Social Security Law

● Require the Social Security Board of Trustees to inform Congress in its annual report if the system is in danger of falling short of funds (before general Treasury revenues can be tapped).

● Require state and local governments to turn over payroll taxes to the Treasury more rapidly. Before the law, such employers could hold the funds for thirty days.

Extension of Coverage

● Require Social Security coverage of all new federal civilian employees, current and future members of Congress, the president, the vice president, sitting federal judges, top political appointees, and civil servants by January 1, 1984.

● Require Social Security coverage of nonprofit organization employees.

● Prohibit state and local governments already under Social Security from withdrawing.

Miscellaneous

● Add two public members to the Social Security Board of Trustees.

● Require a study by April 1, 1984, on how to turn the Social Security Administration into an independent agency.

● Reduce the so-called "windfall benefit" some retirees—most often former government employees—receive when they work under Social Security for only a short time by cutting the base retirement benefit.

● Change the investment procedures of Social Security trust funds to address criticisms that past investments have yielded low returns.

● Credit the Social Security trust funds with certain military benefits and uncashed Social Security checks.

● Restrict benefits for survivors and dependents of nonresident aliens and for convicted felons.

● Include certain elective fringe benefits in the wage base subject to Social Security payroll taxes.

● Eliminate a credit now allowed certain individuals under age sixty-five, who collect government pensions, to compensate them for the fact that their pension income does not include tax-free Social Security benefits.

● Liberalize benefits designed especially to help widowed, divorced, and diabled women; eliminate certain sex distinctions in the law.

would result in a further undermining of public support for the Social Security system. Furthermore, experts generally conceded that any additional revenues derived from increases in the payroll tax alone would not be sufficient to make up the projected Social Security deficit of billions of dollars by the mid-1980s.

Critics of a tax hike pointed out that, with scheduled increases in the payroll tax totaling 15 percent between 1981 and 1990, the average worker's tax burden was too heavy already. Raising Social Security taxes any higher to finance current benefit payments would be unfair to those workers who had to bear the tax burden. Because the tax rate is regressive, increases affect low-income persons disproportionately. On the other hand, since lower-paid workers receive a higher percentage of their past earnings out of the system than better-paid workers, increases in the wage base disproportionately affect the wealthy.

In 1982 there was growing congressional concern about the regressive nature of the Social Security payroll tax because of its great impact on low-income individuals. To relieve the burden of a payroll tax hike, some Democrats proposed an income tax credit for the additional tax paid by low-income individuals.

Another reason commonly given against a payroll tax hike was that it would only serve to slow down the hoped-for economic recovery. Since employers paid half of each employee's Social Security tax, higher tax rates would add to an employer's labor costs and eventually result in increased prices for consumer goods. Some businesses might also be reluctant to hire new workers.

Therefore, higher tax rates could discourage further economic growth. Critics pointed out that this "extra" money eaten up by Social Security taxes perhaps could be used more efficiently elsewhere in the economy, perhaps as capital investments, to spur new growth.

Despite political and economic drawbacks, an increase in the payroll tax was one of the most talked about rescue plans among members of the Greenspan commission.

Under the provisions of the 1977 Social Security changes, workers paid a 6.7 percent payroll tax in 1983, scheduled to increase in increments to 7.65 percent by 1990. Employers would pay the same percentages, bringing the total to 15.3 percent by the end of the decade. According to a staff memo prepared for the commission in September 1982, only by advancing the 1990 tax rate to 1983 would the combined trust funds become "financially viable." But Executive Director Robert J. Myers warned that such an advancement would be "difficult, both legislatively and administratively, let alone politically."

The Congressional Budget Office (CBO) had estimated that moving up the tax increase scheduled for 1990 to 1984 would raise $46 billion. Another possibility was to move up the 1985 and 1986 tax hikes to 1984, which, according to CBO, would raise $17 billion.

Raising taxes had its attractions. As Barber B. Conable, Jr., a member of the Greenspan commission and a Republican representative from New York, pointed out, because there were more than three times as many workers contributing to the Social Security system as there were recipients (including disability and Medicare), changes affecting recipients would hit them three times as hard as changes affecting the system's contributors.

Short of a payroll tax increase, some economists and policy makers suggested that the Social Security payroll tax be reallocated as needed among the three trust funds. One such reallocation—between the DI and OASI funds—was made in 1980. The Greenspan commission considered another reallocation of the payroll tax so that some taxes earmarked for the DI fund—which was expected to have a $171 billion reserve by the end of 1990—would go to OASI instead. In 1981, reallocations of HI funds—to be refunded by general Treasury revenues—had been considered. These would not undermine the "earned right" concept of Social Security, because health-care payments were not strictly tied to past earnings.

General Revenue Financing

Most proposals to use general revenues from the Treasury have been contingency plans to bail out the trust funds when they were in trouble. President Carter in 1978 proposed using income taxes to supplement the payroll tax whenever high unemployment depleted the income of the Social Security trust funds.

The 1979 Advisory Council on Social Security recommended a similar protection against severe economic fluctuations if reserves in the Social Security funds were less than 60 percent of annual outlays.

The National Commission on Social Security advocated that one-half of the cost of Social Security's Health Insurance fund be financed from general revenues, beginning in 1983. Payroll taxes would be kept at the scheduled rates, with the extra money supporting the troubled OASDI (combined) funds. Again, borrowing from the U.S. Treasury could be used as "an emergency measure only."

Most other industrial nations use general revenues to pay for some social insurance, but the idea has been hard to sell to the U.S. Congress. The traditional conservative argument against general revenue financing is that it would obliterate the original insurance theory behind Social Security by breaking the relationship between contributions paid into the system and benefits received.

Opponents of this approach maintained that a Social Security system financed with general tax revenues would be perceived by the public as even more of a welfare program than it already had become. In addition, some lawmakers argued that once general Treasury funds were made available for Social Security financing, it would become very difficult for Congress to resist proposals to increase benefits, thus driving up program costs further.

The main obstacle to all general revenue financing proposals, however, was the federal deficit. Particularly at a time of fiscal austerity, extra money was not been available for a transfer of funds to finance anticipated Social Security deficits.

Some general revenue proposals would take Hospital and Disability Insurance out of the Social Security system and fund them with general Treasury revenues to lessen pressure on the payroll tax.

Removing these programs from the payroll tax would put the OASI fund—for which benefits bear greater relationship to past contributions—on more solid actuarial footing. Such a separation of the welfare and insurance aspects of the Social Security system—with the welfare portions funded from general tax revenues—would allow health and disability payments to be based on need only.

While it would open parts of the system to general revenues, this alternative was designed to overcome the concern that general revenue financing would reduce fiscal discipline in the Social Security program.

While many groups representing the elderly had argued for the use of general revenues in past years, projections about the system's financial condition and the federal budget deficits generally had worsened. In this situation, almost all members of the Greenspan commission agreed that using general revenues was not feasible as a method of rescuing the system. "I think the liberal side would agree that general revenues as a main solution is unlikely to gain acceptance," said Robert Ball, a former Social Security commissioner.

CBO director Alice Rivlin added that relying on "general revenue transfers as the sole means of resolving the Social Security financing problem would place the entire burden of deficit reductions on other portions of the budget." She and Ball suggested the possibility of some limited fallback arrangement allowing Social Security to borrow from the general Treasury in certain emergencies.

The commission thus agreed that some "fail-safe" mechanism should be built into the system in case the changes made to keep it solvent proved insufficient. Myers said such a mechanism could include emergency authority to borrow from general revenues or a "triggered" increase in payroll taxes or COLA cuts if trust fund reserves fell below a certain level.

Increasing Retirement Age

A number of economists and government officials argued that raising the retirement age for full Social Security benefits to sixty-eight or older would resolve to a large extent the system's financial problems. They suggested gradually phasing in the higher age requirement to coincide with the retirement of the baby-boom generation when higher taxes would be needed to pay benefits. According to C. Peter McCollough, chairman of the President's Commission on Pension Policy in 1981, raising the retirement age to sixty-eight would boost the Social Security dependency ratio to four workers to one beneficiary, compared with the projected 2-to-1 ratio by the year 2030.

Advocates of raising the eligibility age argued that sixty-five was an arbitrary age limit, set at a time when life expectancy was considerably shorter. As a result, the burden placed on the system in the 1980s was far beyond what its founders ever imagined. Congress in 1978 raised the mandatory retirement age for most private sector workers to age seventy and abolished the age limit for federal employees. These experts maintained that some adjustment in eligibility for full retirement benefits also was necessary to preserve the integrity of the Social Security system.

The Greenspan commission considered several proposals to slowly increase the retirement age from sixty-five to around sixty-

New Retirement Age and Percentage of Full Benefits Received under 1983 Social Security Law

Age of retirement	Current formula	End of stage one (2009)	End of stage two (2027)
62	80.0%	75.0%	70.0%
63	86.7	80.0	75.0
64	93.3	86.7	80.0
65	100.0	93.3	86.7
66	103.0	100.0	93.3
67	106.0	108.0	100.0

Source: Democratic Study Group, U.S. House of Representatives.

eight. Generally, such proposals called for a hike in the retirement age over a ten-to-twelve-year period early in the twenty-first century. A gradual increase would give workers enough time to take the change into account when making retirement plans.

Another approach to the budgetary advantages of a higher eligibility age was to encourage longer working careers by phasing out the limits in the Social Security program on outside earnings for retired workers age sixty-five to seventy-one. This would provide the system with additional payroll taxes since workers would be paying into the system for longer periods of time and would take out less in benefits later.

The Reagan administration advocated such a policy in 1981. Legislation considered by the House Ways and Means Social Security Subcommittee that year would have eliminated the "earnings test" in 1983 for persons sixty-eight and older. The idea was buried in the general failure of Social Security legislation in 1981, but it was revived in the Senate's 1983 debate on Social Security, eventually becoming law.

Interfund Borrowing

With the idea of general Treasury financing of Social Security benefits so distasteful to so many members of Congress, some experts suggested that the Social Security Administration be given permanent authority to borrow among the three Social Security trust funds. This was a less painful, short-term means of relieving some of Social Security's payment troubles.

This method allowed a fund with a deficit to borrow from a fund with a surplus, easing temporary cash-flow problems. For example, between 1980 and 1982, Congress reallocated some money in the Disability Insurance fund to prop up the ailing OASI fund. Some observers in 1981, including the Congressional Budget Office, indicated that it might tide the system over for ten years or so.

Others, however, including the Social Security Board of Trustees, maintained that interfund borrowing would not provide adequate short-range financing under adverse economic conditions. Any notions of interfund borrowing as the primary remedy to the financing problem were discredited by the time the Greenspan commission issued its report in January 1983.

Yet while the commission and Congress were reluctant to extend interfund borrowing too long because it would threaten depletion of the whole trust fund system, there was some sentiment for allowing OASI to continue borrowing from the healthy DI fund (in addition to the payroll tax reallocation).

Extension of Coverage

Another suggestion for raising new revenues to bail out the Social Security system was through extending coverage to the approximately 2.8 million federal workers and 12 million state and local employees who were not participating in the program before 1983. This group constituted about 10 percent of U.S. workers in 1981.

According to this argument, universal coverage would greatly increase the sys-tem's cashflow in the short run, although most of the anticipated extra revenue eventually would be paid out to a larger number of people drawing benefits. In the long run, according to most analysts, the system probably would not be any better off with the extended coverage.

Legislating universal coverage would prove difficult. Federal workers were regarded as one of the most formidable Washington lobbies. And they obviously had something to fight for: The government pension system was considered far superior to the Social Security system. Initial benefit levels under the federal pension system usually were much higher than those under Social Security or most private pension systems. Federal retirees had the additional security of knowing that—as a matter of routine—their benefits were backed by general Treasury revenues.

However, some thought civil service employees might be amenable to a merger of the two systems if Social Security could be used to supplement certain coverage gaps in their own plans. In 1982, Myers estimated that $21 billion could be raised for the Social Security system during 1983-1989 if all new federal employees (including those with less than five years of service) and employees of nonprofit organizations were required to participate.

Although no specific details were discussed on how such a change would be made, Representative Conable said some procedure could be worked out so that federal employees would still receive supplemental civil service retirement benefits. "No one in the current system would lose out," he vowed.

Left for Congress to consider was a proposal that state and local government employees be required to join the Social Security system. While some commission members favored the idea, it was thought likely to lead to a troublesome constitutional dispute.

Social Security's 'Notch Babies' ...

A quirk in Social Security law has sparked controversy among the nation's elderly, many of whom feel there is a major inequity in the way Social Security recipients are treated.

The story of the "notch babies"—about seven million people born in the "notch" between 1917 and 1921—began in 1972, when lawmakers decided to formalize the ad hoc system of Social Security adjustments they had been using since the program's inception. The automatic cost-of-living adjustments adopted that year as part of a new benefit formula took effect in 1975.

But raging inflation quickly exposed a problem in the new calculation. Because the formula accounted for increases in both wages and prices, Social Security benefits were "overindexed"—that is, they were being boosted twice and were therefore increasing by much more than Congress intended.

For example, some retirees' replacement rates—the percentage of preretirement income that an individual receives as Social Security benefits—soared to nearly 55 percent for some people, well above the 35-38 percent rates that had prevailed until then. Had the trend continued, future retirees would have collected more in monthly retirement benefits than they had earned per month while working.

To correct the problem, Congress in 1977 adopted a new benefit formula for all people born after 1916. The purpose was to stabilize average replacement rates at a level about 5 to 10 percentage points below the rates being approached in 1977, and to shield them from the economic swings that had distorted benefits under the earlier formula.

To cushion the impact on people who were beginning to retire in January 1979, when the new formula was first applied, Congress phased in the change for those born between 1917 and 1921. People born during that period were allowed to use either the new formula or a special transition formula, whichever yielded the higher benefit.

Taxing Benefits

Some experts called for a tax on Social Security benefits as one more method of making the system financially secure. Money derived from such taxes could be channeled back into the trust funds to cover the deficit. Before 1983, Social Security benefits were not subject to federal taxes.

The 1979 Advisory Council on Social Security recommended that 50 percent of benefits be considered as taxable income for federal tax purposes. The advisory council pointed out that instead of a gift, the "right to Social Security benefits is derived from earnings in covered employment just as in the case with private pensions." Private pensions are, of course, subject to federal income tax. Due to the income tax exemptions for the elderly, the council pointed out that even if benefits were subject to taxation, few persons or couples over the age of sixty-five would pay any income tax if Social Security were their only source of income.

The advisory council estimated that, based on 1978 data, taxing half of Social Security benefits would affect 10.6 million tax filings out of the 24.2 million persons who were receiving benefits that year. It

... Stir Up Controversy over Law

But there was another dilemma: What to do about those who were already collecting—and living on—the "windfall" benefits provided under the flawed 1972 formula? Taking money away from these beneficiaries, born between 1910 and 1916, seemed untenable, so Congress decided to let them continue enjoying their bonanza.

This solution had a catch, however. People born in the 1917-1921 notch compared their benefit checks with the retirees born between 1910 and 1916, and not with those born after 1921—those who did not have the option of using the transition formula. Those caught in the notch argue that they are the victims of blatant discrimination by Congress and the Social Security Administration. They say they are being deprived of thousands of dollars in benefits that they have coming to them.

But according to the Social Security Administration and other experts familiar with the notch, the issue is more one of perception than of reality. Although notch babies get smaller monthly benefits than people with similar work histories who were born just before them, the General Accounting Office (GAO), in a report released in March 1988, found that in most cases they were getting more—and never less—than similar retirees who were younger. The GAO also concluded that this situation is entirely in keeping with what Congress intended in 1977 when it changed the Social Security formula to correct the dangerous flaw that was threatening to bankrupt the entire system.

Despite the attention the issue has received, most lawmakers have danced around the idea of "correcting" the notch through legislation. The reason is clear: the cost. Some well-known senior citizens' champions—notably Rep. Claude Pepper, D-Fla., and the American Association of Retired Persons (AARP)—have stayed out of the notch-baby fray. Pepper did not sign on to any of the "correcting" bills introduced, and the AARP long opposed any legislation that would address the notch.

was estimated that the average additional tax would be $350, and the total increase in federal tax collections would be $3.7 billion.

Prospects were slim that Congress would approve the taxation of Social Security benefits. One reason was the obvious political fallout; another was that taxation would change Social Security from a contribution-based to a need-based system. Its critics pointed out that such a tax would be biased against low-income workers, who received a proportionately higher amount of their retirement income from Social Security than those in higher income brackets.

The Greenspan commission, however, did examine the possibility of taxing some portion of Social Security benefits. There was general agreement that any taxing scheme would be imposed only on recipients with incomes above a certain level, easing any burden on low- and middle-income recipients.

According to a CBO study in 1982, if half of all benefits were taxed for individuals with total annual incomes above $20,000, $5.2 billion could be raised over three years. The proposal, not unexpectedly, was extremely unpopular with the public. Pollster Louis Harris told the Senate Finance Committee in September 1982 that

86 percent of those interviewed in a poll had opposed any taxation of Social Security benefits.

Other Tax Proposals

Other suggestions for raising additional revenue for the Social Security system through taxation received comparatively little attention. A plan offered by Sen. John C. Danforth, R-Mo., would have added a 10-cent tax to a package of cigarettes to raise revenues for the Health Insurance trust fund. Others suggested easing the burden of future Social Security costs with a "value-added tax," which essentially was a national sales tax levied on manufacturers at each stage in the production and distribution of a particular product.

Efforts in the Ninety-seventh Congress to bolster the Social Security system through revenues derived from the tax on oil industry profits resulting from the 1981 deregulation of oil received little support. Moreover, the Reagan administration was adamantly opposed to increasing taxes for Social Security.

In 1982 proposals resembling those of Senator Danforth to increase the excise taxes on products such as alcohol and tobacco for the HI and DI trust funds again came under consideration. The rationale was that since such products are considered health risks, users should pay additional fees to fund the government programs that pay benefits for health and disability care. One drawback, however, was that tobacco taxes had just been raised earlier in 1982, and plans for additional levies were sure to face heavy industry and congressional opposition.

Spending Cuts

The alternative to increasing revenues was to cut outlays. Expenditures for administering the trust funds could be reduced

somewhat, or benefit payments could be decreased by either cutting them across-the-board or tightening eligibility requirements.

Some observers maintained that one way to reduce spending was to reduce waste and fraud in the administration of the Social Security program. The Social Security Administration had been criticized for its heavy case backlog and chronic computer problems.

The investment policies of the Social Security trust funds also had been blamed for the shortfalls. Sen. William Proxmire, D-Wis., charged that Social Security "needlessly" lost $2 billion in 1980 by investing in securities that yielded low—8.3 percent—interest. He introduced a measure in the Ninety-seventh Congress to require the system's Board of Trustees to maximize its investments.

New Benefit Formulas

In the Ninety-seventh Congress there was strong support for changing the formulas by which Social Security benefits were indexed. One Reagan administration proposal that received widespread attention would have cut benefits for future retirees. The plan entailed a revision of the formula used to determine the monthly payment for a retiree.

Again in 1982, a change in the indexing formula was proposed so that workers would have a lower "replacement rate." Benefits would not actually be cut, instead they would not increase by as much as they had under prevailing law. This plan eventually was superseded by proposals to adjust cost-of-living allowances as the main benefit reduction considered by the Greenspan commission.

COLA Changes

Many experts had called for changes in the indexing of annual cost-of-living increases in Social Security benefits. Under the pre-1983 law, Social Security benefits

Tax Rates before and after
1983 Social Security Law

Year	Prior law	New law
1983	6.70%	6.70%
1984	6.70	6.70/7.00[a]
1985	7.05	7.05
1986	7.15	7.15
1987	7.15	7.15
1988	7.15	7.51
1989	7.15	7.51
1990	7.65	7.65

Source: Democratic Study Group, U.S. House of Representatives.

[a] In 1984, employees continued to pay taxes at the 6.7% rate, with an additional 0.3% provided from general revenues; employers paid taxes at the 7.0% rate.

were increased each July by 100 percent of the rise in the Consumer Price Index during the previous year. The Reagan administration proposed in 1981 that the annual cost-of-living increases be moved to October of each year, to coincide with the beginning of the government's fiscal year. Expected savings for the three-month delay for fiscal 1982-1986 would be about $6.3 billion, according to the administration.

For members of the Greenspan commission, the attraction of a COLA cut was that its effects would be cumulative. If the COLA was reduced by a few percentage points one year, for example, then increases in subsequent years would be smaller as a result. There were a number of COLA-adjustment options available to the commission. A one-time move of the COLA payment from July to October would result in a savings of $7 billion through 1985, according to CBO. Another proposal before the commission was to cap the increase at a certain percentage, such as 4 percent, for a savings of $7.7 billion over the same period.

Opponents of the COLA proposals, however, pointed out that, while some retirees no doubt were well off, millions were on the verge of poverty. Each reduction in COLA increases, they said, could have profound financial effects. According to a study commissioned by the American Association of Retired Persons, capping the COLA at two-thirds of the increase in prices, beginning in 1983, would force 500,000 elderly below the poverty line by 1985 and 1.3 million by 1990.

The CBO's Rivlin suggested that such problems could be accommodated in part by liberalizing benefits and eligibility requirements of the welfare-oriented Supplemental Security Income program.

Insulation from Inflation

Many economists maintained that the CPI distorted the real level of inflation and that fluctuations in the economy had disproportionate effects upon the Social Security trust funds. The increase in prices relative to wages was the main factor behind this imbalance.

A number of Social Security advisory groups, along with Senate Budget Committee chairman Pete V. Domenici, R-N.M., and economist Martin Feldstein, who served as chairman of the President's Council of Economic Advisers during the Reagan administration, proposed various mechanisms to insulate Social Security from movements of the CPI in 1981. These ranged from the indexation of benefits to the lower of annual average increase in prices or wages to capping COLA increases at some point below increases in the CPI.

Myers developed a proposal for the Greenspan commission that tied future benefit increases to wages instead of to prices, as they had been since 1977. His plan called for a formula in which the COLA benefit would reflect an increase in the wage level minus 1.5 percent—a figure actuaries used for their long-term projections of price increases when calculating future COLAs. "If in 1977 we had geared benefit increases to the lesser of wages and prices, we wouldn't be sitting here talking today," he said. "What it [the proposed formula] does is ask beneficiaries to have a share in the economy. If it's bad, you have to suffer a little; if it's good you can benefit."

Eventually, the commission recommended automatic COLA adjustments to wages or prices—depending on which of the two had increased less in the preceding year—if the funds' reserve ratios dipped below 15 percent.

Medicare and Medicaid

When Congress established a medical care system for the aged through the Social Security system in 1965, the federal government assumed substantial responsibility for paying the health-care bills of the nation's elderly and poor. Under the system's main component, Medicare, today virtually all Americans age sixty-five and over, regardless of income level, are entitled to hospital benefits. A voluntary supplementary Medicare policy covers 80 percent of many other medical costs, including physicians' fees.

The other part of the U.S. health-care system, Medicaid, is a public assistance program differing from Medicare in that it uses a combination of state and federal funds—instead of federal funds alone—to provide medical care for the poor. Each state is required to provide health care conforming to federal standards to those who qualify for public assistance but sets the amount of benefits on its own.

The Medicare and Medicaid programs have been largely successful in meeting the health-care needs of the elderly and poor. The elderly have benefited from both programs. Medicare provides hospital protection for 95 percent of that group, while Medicaid specifically helps the elderly poor pay for services not covered by Medicare, such as nursing-home care.

Better health care for the elderly and poor has been expensive, however. The federal programs have been plagued by some of the same problems confronting the private health-care sector, especially rising costs and program abuses.

As with private insurance, Medicare and Medicaid as originally created provided payments to health-care providers—hospitals, doctors, and skilled nursing facilities—after costs were incurred. This gave providers and patients few incentives to keep costs down.

At the same time, the agencies that run Medicare and Medicaid have also been victims of outright fraud—billed by health-care providers for services not rendered or for patients not seen. To a lesser extent, patients have made fraudulent statements about their eligibility.

Enactment of Medicare and Medicaid in 1965, as part of President Lyndon B. Johnson's Great Society program, reflected the view in Congress and in the administration that access to health care was the right of all Americans. Developments in the early 1970s furthered this idea by expanding benefits and loosening eligibility requirements.

But almost from their inception the programs proved to be much more expensive than planners had envisioned. The rising costs of health care that accompanied inflation throughout the 1970s led to a number of belt-tightening measures late in that decade. Congress curtailed benefits—increasing the share of health costs beneficiaries had to pay themselves—and tightened eligibility requirements. In recent years, major efforts have been made to detach Medicaid eligibility from welfare eligibility.

By the 1980s, cost control was the principal issue of the health-care debate. Painful choices will have to be made in the search for a new balance between the costs and benefits of more federal spending on medical care. A major challenge to policy makers of the future will be to stem the flow of health-cost burdens from one group of institutions to another. And just as some objected to certain reforms proposed and enacted for being insufficiently comprehensive, others believed that unless health policy was formulated for all segments of the population and not just the elderly, cost containment would not be achieved.

Background

In 1798, Congress established a government health-insurance program for the merchant marine, perhaps the first such program in the United States. Sailors were required to contribute a few cents a month to pay for hospital care provided by a marine hospital. It was not until the early twentieth century, however, that the idea of compulsory health insurance for the general public gained serious attention. The debate was spurred by the American Association for Labor Legislation (AALL), a group of lawyers, academics, and other professionals that lobbied in several states for enactment of health-insurance legislation.

Meanwhile, after publishing several articles in favor of compulsory health insurance, the American Medical Association

(AMA) drafted health-insurance bills that were introduced in the New York and Massachusetts legislatures. In 1917 the AMA's House of Delegates endorsed a health-insurance plan comparable to an earlier bill drafted by the AALL.

Opposition to the idea of compulsory health insurance developed almost immediately. The opponents were in large part labor leaders, including Samuel Gompers, who felt that a national health-insurance system would result in government control over the working class. In addition, they feared that such an insurance plan would cause fewer employees to join unions and give management a reason for not granting raises.

Employers also opposed compulsory health insurance for fear they would have to contribute a disproportionate share of funding to the plan. By 1920 the AMA, reacting to pressure from state medical societies, had reversed its position and opposed compulsory health insurance.

Inspiration of Social Security

Interest in a government-sponsored health program was not revived until the 1930s, when the Great Depression stimulated greater concern for social welfare. The Social Security Act of 1935 established a broad range of social insurance and public assistance programs.

Although the Social Security Act did not include a health-insurance program, the president's Committee on Economic Security had endorsed the principle of compulsory national health insurance. Roosevelt dropped the idea for fear its inclusion in the 1935 legislation would endanger passage of the entire act.

Medical expenses were taken into account in determining an individual's monthly payments under Social Security's public assistance programs. However, financial support for medical services was a small part of welfare assistance since participation by the states in these programs was optional.

From 1935 on, compulsory health-insurance bills were introduced regularly in Congress. One of the most comprehensive was that proposed in 1943 by Sens. Robert F. Wagner, D-N.Y. (1927-1949), James E. Murray, D-Mont. (1934-1961), and Rep. John D. Dingell, D-Mich. (1933-1955). The Wagner-Murray-Dingell bill called for a sweeping revision of the Social Security Act, including the creation of a compulsory national health-insurance system for persons of all ages to be administered by the federal government and financed through a payroll tax. No action was taken on the measure in the Seventy-eighth Congress, however, and the proposal died.

In 1945 President Harry S Truman, in a message to Congress, proposed a comprehensive medical insurance plan for all persons to be financed through a 4 percent increase in the Social Security Act's Old Age and Survivors Insurance tax. Truman recommended that the plan cover doctor, hospital, nursing, laboratory, and dental services.

Lobbying on the Truman proposal reached a peak when the president pushed for congressional action in 1949-1950. Labor unions supported national health insurance but could not overcome the opposition of the AMA, the private health-insurance industry, and business groups. Ultimately, the AMA's dire warnings that national health insurance would mean "socialized medicine" and government interference in medical practice made Congress wary of the measure, and there was no action in either chamber.

Incremental Progress

Although Congress refused to take action on compulsory health insurance, it did move in 1950 to help states provide medical assistance to welfare recipients through amendments to the Social Security law. The amendments provided federal support to the states to cover part of the costs of vendor payments (direct reimbursement to hospitals and clinics) for the health care of persons eligible for any of the following four federal-state programs: Old Age Assistance (OAA), Aid to Dependent Children (ADC), Aid to the Blind (AB), and Aid to the Permanently and Totally Disabled (APTD). Federal sharing of the costs greatly accelerated state efforts in health care for public assistance recipients.

In 1952, after it had become clear that Truman's proposal for compulsory health insurance was not likely to be passed soon, if ever, some of its congressional backers suggested a less comprehensive plan. They proposed that the Social Security Old-Age and Survivors Insurance system (OASI) begin paying for the hospitalization costs of retired persons receiving OASI old-age benefits. Their plan was directed at assisting elderly persons who had high health-care costs and low incomes, and thus could not afford the high premiums of commercial health insurance.

There was no congressional action on the hospital cost payment plan while Truman was president, and the Eisenhower administration, which came to office in 1953, opposed the concept of compulsory health insurance. But in 1957 legislation was introduced by Rep. Aime J. Forand, D-R.I. (1937-1939, 1941-1961), that incorporated many features of the 1952 plan. Forand's proposal covered hospital, nursing home, and surgical costs of the aged, financed by an increase in the OASI payroll tax. There was little congressional activity on the issue until 1960, but the Forand plan drew considerable public interest.

By 1960 the Forand bill had become an intensely partisan issue, with the chief interest groups taking positions similar to those they had taken a decade earlier on Truman's comprehensive health-care proposals. Backing the bill were organized labor, Democrats, and liberal groups. Against the bill were most Republicans, including President Eisenhower, and spokespersons for business and insurance groups.

Once again, the AMA conducted a nationwide lobbying campaign against compulsory medical insurance. The Eisenhower administration responded with its own program to help the needy aged meet the costs of catastropic illness without compulsory national health insurance.

In Congress, however, the House Ways and Means Committee opted for a plan similar to, but less generous than, Eisenhower's. Congress eventually amended the Social Security Act along these lines when it passed the Kerr-Mills bill in July 1960. The bill was named for sponsors Wilbur D. Mills, D-Ark. (1939-1977), chairman of the House Ways and Means committee, and Sen. Robert S. Kerr, D-Okla. (1949-1963).

The Kerr-Mills bill extended the 1950 Social Security amendments by providing additional federal funds to the states for vendor payments under the Old Age Assistance program. It also established the Medical Assistance to the Aged (MAA) program, which was a separate federal matching grant program for the needy aged who were not receiving cash assistance. Under this program the government agreed to reimburse states for 50 to 80 percent of the cost of setting up state programs to pay medical costs for needy aged persons.

A Procedural Obstacle

John F. Kennedy, first as a senator (D-Mass., 1953-1960) and then as president (1961-1963), strongly backed the concept of health insurance for the aged. Shortly after taking office, President Kennedy proposed to Congress a revised version of the Forand plan to be introduced by Rep. Cecil R. King, D-Calif. (1942-1969), and Sen. Clin-

ton P. Anderson, D-N.M. (1949-1973). The new health-care proposal called for Social Security coverage for ninety days of hospital care (with a small deductible), extensive nursing-home care, or home health services, but it did not provide for payment of surgical costs.

But while the King-Anderson bill was an annual presidential priority from 1961 through 1964, administration efforts were frustrated throughout this period. One factor in these failures was a constitutional rule requiring that any revenue-raising bills—including amendments to the Social Security Act—originate in the House. In practice this meant that Social Security bills had to be reported from the House Ways and Means Committee if they were to have any chance of enactment. Unfortunately for proponents of health insurance, that committee was controlled by its powerful chairman, Wilbur Mills.

Naturally the administration took every opportunity to convince the House leadership to fill Ways and Means Committee vacancies with members who would support health insurance for the aged. In 1963 the margin of opposition on the committee had declined to one member, but Mills stood firm against the plan and administration efforts to get a majority behind the bill failed.

Mills's disapproval of Social Security involvement in medical care for the aged was considered a major stumbling block to such a program by 1964. Mills elaborated his views that year in a speech in Little Rock, Ark.:

> Many of the newspapers have widely reported that, singlehandedly, I have for six or seven years prevented this legislation from being considered.... Apparently a majority of the members of the House of Representatives share the deep concern which I have over using the Old Age, Survivors and Disability Insurance (OASDI) system for financing a medical or hospital

Terminology Used in the Medicare Program

Following are definitions of terms used in the Medicare program, the federally funded medical care system for the elderly. *(See also Glossary of Terms Used in Debate over Catastrophic Health Insurance, box, p. 68)*

Copayment (also called coinsurance)—The dollar amount of services covered under the Medicare program that a patient is responsible for paying (beyond the deductible amount the patient also must pay).

Deductible—The initial dollar amount that the patient must pay for medical services before Medicare insurance payments begin.

Assignment—A method of medical insurance payment in which reimbursement for services rendered is made by Medicare to a doctor or supplier. When the assignment method is used, the doctor or supplier agrees that the total charge for the covered service will be the amount approved by the Medicare carrier.

Balance Billing (also called charge reductions)—The amount, in addition to the required coinsurance, for which beneficiaries are liable when a supplier does not accept assignment. If, for example, a doctor charges $100 for a service for which Medicare's approved charge is only $50, the patient would be responsible for the required 20 percent coinsurance (since Medicare Part B pays 80 percent of the charge) as well as the "balance" between what Medicare recognizes and what the physician charges, in this case, another $50.

Carriers—Private insurance companies that handle claims from doctors and other suppliers of services covered under Medicare's supplementary medical insurance program (part B).

Intermediaries—Private insurance companies under contract with the government that handle Medicare claims (part A) from hospitals, skilled-nursing facilities, and home health agencies.

Providers—Doctors, "allied" health professionals (such as physical therapists), hospitals, skilled-nursing facilities, or home health facilities that provide medical services to Medicare beneficiaries.

"Reasonable Charges" (also called approved charges)—The portion of the total cost of a given medical service to be borne by Medicare, as deemed appropriate by the Medicare carrier. The amount of the charge—reviewed annually—is based on whichever is lowest, the physician's customary charge, the prevailing charge in the region, or, in the event of services already rendered, the actual charge.

"Reasonable Costs"—The provider costs for services to Medicare beneficiaries. These costs are determined on the basis of an annual cost report from the provider and are paid only to the provider (not the patient).

Suppliers—Persons or organizations, other than doctors or health care facilities, that furnish equipment or services covered by Medicare insurance. Ambulance firms, independent laboratories, and organizations that rent or sell medical equipment are considered suppliers.

care program. . . .

I have always maintained that at some point there is a limit to the amount of a worker's wages, or the earnings of a self-employed person, that can reasonably be expected to finance the Social Security system. . . . The central fact which must be faced on a proposal to provide a form of service benefit—as contrasted with a cash benefit—is that it is very difficult to accurately estimate the cost. These difficult-to-predict future costs, when such a program is part of the Social Security program, could well have highly dangerous ramifications on the cash benefits portion of the Social Security system. The American people must be assured of the continued soundness of the OASDI program.

Although the King-Anderson proposals passed the Senate for the first time in 1964 as an amendment to a bill raising Social Security retirement benefits, the bill died in conference when a majority of House conferees opposed any medical care plan.

Assembling a Compromise

Failure of the King-Anderson bill in 1964 was, up until that time, one of President Johnson's few serious legislative defeats. In 1965, therefore, he took no risks. The president's first legislative message to the Eighty-ninth Congress dealt with health legislation. In it he called 1965 the year "when, with the sure knowledge of public support, the Congress should enact a hospital insurance program for the aged. . . . In this way, the spectre of catastrophic hospital bills can be lifted from the lives of our older citizens."

Johnson's 1965 hospital care bill was very similar to those that had been introduced and debated since 1961. One major difference, however, was that the new bill provided coverage for sixty days of hospital care, instead of ninety days. Other major provisions called for the following benefits: sixty days of nursing-home care, 240 home

health-care visits, and outpatient hospital diagnostic services. The program covered all persons sixty-five and over, except government workers with federal insurance and certain aliens. It was to be financed mainly by increases in the Social Security tax rate.

The AMA once again mounted a vigorous campaign against the administration proposals, but this time changed its strategy by attacking the bill for not being sufficiently comprehensive. The medical association argued that the elderly needed more than just hospital benefits. They introduced an alternative plan, called "eldercare," which covered doctor bills. The eldercare plan called for a voluntary comprehensive medical insurance program that would be available to persons sixty-five and over if their state government signed up for the program. The program was to be financed by matching federal-state funds and variable contributions from recipients.

The House Republican leadership also set forth their own bill, introduced by the ranking minority member of the Ways and Means Committee, John W. Byrnes, R-Wis. (1945-1973). The Byrnes bill provided a voluntary health-insurance program for all persons sixty-five and over, which would cover a large proportion of most health-care costs in old age. It was to be administered by the federal government and financed by a graduated premium contribution based on the individual's ability to pay, by contributions from the states, and by an annual appropriations from the federal government.

All three plans—the administration proposal, the Byrnes bill, and the AMA's eldercare plan—contributed to the medical care bill that finally was enacted in 1965. Chairman Mills had an influential role in both the shaping and the passage of the legislation.

Mills's change of heart was interpreted as a reflection of his unwillingness to be on the losing side of an issue. Theodore

Marmor in *The Politics of Medicare*, published in 1970, said: "Mills' conception of himself as the active head of an autonomous, technically expert committee helps explain his interest in shaping legislation he could no longer block, and his preoccupation with cautious financing of the Social Security system made him willing to combine benefit and financing arrangements that had been presented as mutually exclusive alternatives."

Today's Programs Take Shape

As passed by Congress July 28, 1965, the Health Insurance for the Aged Act (PL 89-97) added two new titles (XVIII and XIX) to the Social Security Act. Part A of Title XVIII was basically the King-Anderson bill; it provided persons over sixty-five with insurance to cover the costs of hospital and related care. The program was to be financed by a Social Security trust fund, to which employers and employees were required to contribute. Part B of Title XVIII drew heavily on the Byrnes bill and called for a voluntary system of supplemental medical insurance covering doctors' fees and certain other health services.

Title XIX, the Medicaid section of the bill, provided a program of federal matching grants to states that chose to make medical services available to welfare recipients and the medically indigent.

Basic Health Insurance

Most persons age sixty-five and older became eligible for the basic health insurance program (part A) when the law took effect in 1966. Not eligible were active or retired federal employees enrolled in the federal health benefits program, aliens who had not been lawfully admitted for permanent status or had not lived in the United

States for at least five consecutive years, and persons convicted of certain crimes.

The plan provided the following benefits:

● Inpatient hospital services for up to ninety days for each period of illness, with the patient paying a deductible amount of $40 for the first sixty days and $10 a day for the next thirty days. Each patient was eligible for sixty nonrenewable days of inpatient hospital services (beyond the ninety-day period) in his lifetime. Excluded from covered inpatient care were the services of radiologists, anesthesiologists, pathologists, and physiatrists. Also excluded were private duty nursing and hospital services of physicians, except services provided by dental and medical interns and residents under approved teaching programs. Psychiatric hospital care was subject to a lifetime limit of 190 days, with 60 days per illness.

● Posthospital care for up to one hundred days for each period of illness after at least three days in the hospital, with the patient paying $5 a day after the first twenty days. (Nursing homes delivering "skilled" as opposed to "intermediate" care were considered posthospital facilities.)

● Outpatient diagnostic services, with the patient paying the first $20 for diagnostic services provided by the same hospital during a twenty-day period and 20 percent of the remaining costs. The $20 deductible was credited against the annual $50 deductible required under the supplementary health plan.

● Up to one hundred home health-care visits by a nurse or physician's assistant after discharge from at least a three-day stay in hospital, or from an extended-care facility, and before the beginning of a new period of illness.

The plan defined a period of illness as beginning when the patient entered a hospital or a nursing home and ending when the patient had not been hospitalized for sixty consecutive days. (This "spell of illness" concept remained in effect until the adoption of the catastrophic health insurance bill in 1988.)

Part A also provided that deductions required for the various services would be increased if necessary to meet rising health-care costs and that payment to providers of the services would cover the "reasonable cost" of the services.

The plan was to be financed by a payroll tax, which would apply equally to employers, employees, and self-employed persons. The tax was fixed at 0.35 percent in 1966, 0.50 percent in 1967-1972, 0.60 percent in 1976-1979, 0.70 percent in 1980-1986, and 0.80 percent in 1987 and thereafter. (Later changes ultimately boosted the rate to 1.45 percent for 1986 and thereafter.)

The annual taxable earnings base for the health-insurance payroll tax was the same as that for Social Security's old age and disability insurance funds, $6,600. The plan provided that general revenues would finance the plan for persons not covered by Social Security or the Railroad Retirement Act.

Health-insurance payroll taxes (and general revenue funds for those not covered by Social Security) for the plan were to go into a separate Hospital Insurance (HI) trust fund in the Treasury Department.

The secretary of the Department of Health, Education and Welfare (HEW) was to administer the basic health-insurance plan.

Supplementary Medical Care

The initial enrollment period for the supplementary plan (part B) for persons age sixty-five and older was set as a seven-month period beginning three months before the sixty-fifth birthday. No person could enroll after three years from the close of the first period in which he was eligible to enroll. Persons who dropped out of the plan could reenroll only once, and it had to be within three years of dropping out. The plan provided that states could enroll and pay the premiums of their public assistance recipients.

The benefits provided that the supplementary plan would pay 80 percent of the patient's costs, after an annual deductible of $50, on the following:

● Services of physicians, surgeons, radiologists, anesthesiologists, pathologists, and psychiatrists, and certain services of dental surgeons, regardless of whether these services were provided in a hospital, clinic, office, or home.

● Up to one hundred home health-care visits a calendar year.

● Other medical and health services, whether provided in or out of a medical institution, including X-rays, laboratory tests, electrocardiograms, basal metabolism readings, artificial legs, arms and eyes, and rental of certain medical equipment. Payment for out-of-hospital mental disorders would be limited in each calendar year to $250 or 50 percent of the costs, whichever was smaller. Payment would not be made for routine exams, dental care, eyeglasses, or hearing aids.

The plan required that payments to institutional providers be based on "reasonable costs" and payments to doctors be based on "reasonable charges."

The supplementary medical insurance plan was to be financed jointly by persons enrolled in the plan and by the federal government. Enrollees would pay monthly premiums of $3 each. The premiums would be deducted from the monthly retirement benefits received under the Social Security, railroad, and civil retirement systems. The federal government would match from general revenues the $3 monthly premium paid by each enrollee. Individual and government contributions went into a separate trust fund for the supplementary insurance plan.

alth services under Medicare and payent for minor surgery or tests done outside ospitals. Existing law ordinarily covered ese services only if the patient was hospilized.

Other changes made by the reconciliaon bill were meant to encourage physians not to charge their elderly patients ore than Medicare would pay for certain ervices, but these provisions were not made andatory. Under existing law, doctors uld, and often did, charge well above hat the program considered a "reasonble" fee, and patients had to pay the fference.

Reducing the Government's Role

Ronald Reagan was elected president 1980 on a pledge to reduce the role of the deral government. As a candidate, he dorsed the concept of health insurance in e event of a catastrophe but flatly rected a national health-insurance plan. He bscribed to a "free-market" or "competion" health policy based on a theory dvocated by Alain C. Enthoven, a Stanrd University economist specializing in e study of health care. The idea behind a ee-market health plan was that if individls spent their own health dollars, they uld demand and get better and cheaper rvices. Cost and quality would be largely ntrolled by market forces, not governent regulators.

Reagan's First Two Years

Most changes in the Medicare and edicaid programs during Reagan's first o years were part of a larger administraon effort to cut spending for social proams and to reduce the federal deficit. owever, administration officials also ught to create pressure for a future overhaul of health-care financing in the United States. Ultimately, said HHS Secretary Richard S. Schweiker, the administration wanted to "use the marketplace to hold down these costs," instead of relying on spending limits and other regulations imposed by Congress.

Medicaid Cuts/Local Autonomy

Congress agreed to cut federal Medicaid spending in 1981 but rejected a Reagan administration proposal to set a rigid ceiling on federal Medicaid contributions to the states. The Economic Recovery Tax Act of that year (PL 97-35) required reductions in spending for Medicaid (3 percent in fiscal 1982, 4 percent in fiscal 1983, and 4.5 percent in fiscal 1984). Those cuts were expected to reduce federal spending on the programs by $5.8 billion.

The 1981 bill also broadened the independent authority of the states under Medicaid, modifying a provision of the 1965 Act allowing Medicaid recipients to choose their own health-care providers (doctors, hospitals, and skilled-nursing facilities), and giving states the option of restricting physicians and facilities available to recipients in certain cases. States would also be able to arrange for laboratory services or procure medical devices through competitive bidding.

Perhaps the most important provision was one that gave the states the opportunity to waive restrictions on the types of services the federal government would fund through Medicaid reimbursements. Previously, Medicaid insurance for certain treatments or procedures had been restricted to inpatient stays. The Medicaid waivers provided a mechanism by which states could be reimbursed for providing home- and community-based health services to recipients who otherwise would have had to seek more expensive hospital or nursing-home care to qualify for federal payments.

According to the Intergovernmental

Gross National Product and National Health Expenditures, Selected Years, 1929-1986

| Year | Gross national product (in billions) | National health expenditures | | |
		Amount (in billions)	Percentage of gross national product	Amount per capita
1929	$ 103.9	$ 3.6	3.5	$ 29
1935	72.8	2.9	4.0	23
1940	100.4	4.0	4.0	29
1950	288.3	12.7	4.4	80
1955	405.9	17.7	4.4	101
1960	515.3	26.9	5.2	142
1965	705.1	41.9	5.9	205
1966	772.0	46.3	6.0	224
1967	816.4	51.5	6.3	247
1968	892.6	58.2	6.5	276
1969	963.9	65.6	6.8	309
1970	1,015.5	75.0	7.4	349
1971	1,102.7	83.5	7.6	384
1972	1,212.8	94.0	7.7	428
1973	1,359.3	103.4	7.6	467
1974	1,472.8	116.1	7.9	521
1975	1,598.4	132.7	8.3	590
1976	1,782.8	150.8	8.5	665
1977	1,990.5	169.9	8.5	743
1978	2,249.7	189.7	8.4	822
1979	2,508.2	214.7	8.6	921
1980	2,731.9	248.1	9.1	1,054
1981	3,052.6	287.0	9.4	1,207
1982	3,166.0	323.6	10.2	1,348
1983	3,405.7	357.2	10.5	1,473
1984	3,765.0	391.1	10.4	1,597
1985	3,998.1	422.6	10.6	1,710
1986	4,206.1	458.2	10.9	1,837

Source: Health Care Financing Administration.
Note: These data, compiled by the Health Care Financing Administration, reflect Bureau of Economic Analysis, Department of Commerce, revisions to the gross national product as of December 1986 and Social Security Administration revisions to the population as of April 1986.

The plan provided that the premium could be increased as medical costs rose. A higher premium was also levied on those persons who delayed enrollment until after the first period when enrollment was open to them and for persons who reenrolled after dropping out.

The secretary of HEW would contract with private carriers to perform major administrative functions of the plan, such as determining rates of payments and disbursing funds.

Medicaid

The medical provisions for the needy already covered under the Social Security Act were combined in a new title (XIX) to the act, which became known as Medicaid. The plan also extended the Medical Assistance for the Aged (MAA) program for the indigent aged to needy persons under the dependent children, blind, and permanently and totally disabled programs; and made eligible for medical aid needy children who did not qualify for public assistance (if the state so provided). Existing provisions of the act covering medical assistance programs would terminate upon adoption of the new program.

States participating in the program were required to provide inpatient and outpatient hospital services, laboratory and X-ray services, skilled nursing home services, and physicians' services. States could provide additional benefits. Needy persons receiving state aid were to be provided with assistance to meet the deductible amounts imposed by the federal basic health plan.

The plan increased the federal share under the existing MAA federal-state matching program so that states with average per capita incomes would receive 55 percent (instead of the existing 50 percent) and states with very low per capita incomes could receive up to 83 percent (instead of 80 percent).

The federal government was required to pick up a 75 percent share of the cost of training professional medical personnel participating in the programs and 50 percent of the other administrative expenses.

States were required to provide a means test to determine eligibility of the needy elderly for the program. The program would not be based on rigid income standards, which could adversely affect persons of some means but with very large medical bills.

1967-1980 Adjustments

From 1967 to 1980 federal expenditures for health care rose with the expansion of the Medicare and Medicaid programs. Congress expanded both eligibility and the variety of services covered. Almost at the start of the programs, it was realized that they were more costly than planners had envisioned. While the Nixon and Ford administrations were concerned about cost containment, Congress did little to curb

program expenditures.

During the period 1967-1977, national compulsory health insurance remained a controversial issue and an elusive goal. While the Nixon and Carter administrations paid lip service to some form of national health insurance, their actual proposals were more limited, with an emphasis on catastrophic health insurance. Even that goal was not realized until 1988.

However, a number of intermediate developments in health insurance occurred in these years. Specifically, certain benefit extensions in the Medicare and Medicaid programs in the 1970s reflected a new emphasis on preventive medicine and less expensive forms of health care, such as health maintenance organizations (HMOs) and home health services.

New Programs/Physicians' Review

Nixon's 1971 health-insurance proposal had three parts: a national health-insurance standards program designed to fill the gap caused by the failure of many private insurance plans to cover catastrophic illness costs; a federal Family Health Insurance Plan to replace Medicaid; and a proposal to encourage the development of HMOs, which provided prepaid comprehensive health care. Despite extensive hearings in House and Senate committees, Congress did not act on these proposals in 1971 or 1972.

However, major alterations of the Medicare and Medicaid program were included in legislation enacted in 1972 (PL 92-603) revising the Social Security Act. The main provisions of that law extended Medicare eligibility to an additional 1.7 million disabled Social Security beneficiaries; provided federal funding for Medicare beneficiaries to enroll in HMOs that provided federally approved services; brought the services of chiropractors under Medicare; provided coverage under Medicare for most Americans afflicted with chronic kid-

ney disease; and established professional standards review organizations (PSROs)—representing local practicing physicians—to oversee Medicaid and Medicare services.

During the Ninety-third Congress (1973-1975), several measures were enacted that coordinated Medicaid eligibility requirements with the federal Supplemental Security Income (SSI) program, which provided federal assistance to the needy aged, blind, and disabled. One part of Nixon's 1971 national health-insurance program—federal assistance to HMOs—was passed by Congress in December 1973, in a more limited form than the original proposal.

In 1975 legislation was passed (PL 94-182) that extended the time limit for local medical groups to set up PSROs. That law also provided that prevailing charges for physician services under Medicare could not be lowered. HEW regulations had tied increases in Medicare reimbursement rates to an economic index, and the 1975 measure represented a legislative victory for medical groups.

Management Reforms

Originally, a number of different HEW bureaus and divisions administered the Medicare and Medicaid programs. In 1977 their functions were consolidated and transferred to the Health Care Financing Administration, which was established in March 1977 as part of HEW. (HEW officially went out of existence May 4, 1980, and was replaced by two departments: the Department of Health and Human Services (HHS) and the Department of Education.)

In 1976 and 1977 Congress moved to correct mismanagement in the two programs when it passed legislation (PL 95-142) increasing penalties for fraud and abuse, strengthening the oversight responsibilities of PSROs, and requiring more ownership information from providers. The bill was the result of three years of congressional study that followed disclosure by

federal and state investigat backs, fraudulent billings, medical treatment, and ot were occurring in the federa grams. (Congress in 1976 al an Office of Inspector Gene (now HHS).)

In 1977 Congress approv (PL 95-210) that extended M Medicaid reimbursement to vided by nurse practitioners an assistants in rural clinics. The designed to encourage the deve utilization of rural health clin cally underserved areas. In 197 was enacted (PL 95-292) that kidney disease program under provide incentives for patients kidney dialysis treatments in the alternative to more costly ho dialysis.

Carter Plan Stymied

Carter had made a com health-insurance proposal one paign pledges, but his 1979 pr limited to a catastrophic healt program. Carter's plan was not a Congress due in part to concern cost of the plan.

Perhaps more importantly, House and its allies—the insura try, organized labor, and groups ing the elderly—were out-lobbi catastrophic health insurance w many priorities for those groups, and the hospital lobby worked a plan without distraction.

The following year, however, of changes were made in Medi Medicaid as a part of the fiscal 198 reconciliation bill (PL 96-499). (budget act provided for a "recon procedure for bringing the overall by the federal government into co with the spending decisions made gress.) The bill expanded coverage

Health Policy Project (IHPP), a university health-research project funded by the Health Care Financing Administration, forty states applied for waivers between October 1981 and May 1983. Meanwhile, more than thirty states cut back on types of benefits, eligibility groups, and payments under Medicaid in 1981, according to the IHPP.

Additional savings would come from increases in the deductible payments required of Medicare beneficiaries for both the basic (part A) and supplementary (part B) insurance programs, and from other limits on reimbursements.

A Second Round of Cuts

Congress made a number of further changes in Medicare and Medicaid in the Tax Equity and Fiscal Responsibility Act of 1982 (PL 97-248)—President Reagan's tax increase measure—in an effort to reduce federal outlays for health programs in fiscal 1983-1985. The changes would cut spending for the programs by an estimated $14.4 billion over the three years, nearly two and one-half times the amount pruned from the programs in 1981.

The bulk of the spending reductions made by the 1982 act came in Medicare ($13.3 billion). The principal cost-cutting measures revised limits on payments to hospitals and doctors. One provision imposed new caps on the percentage of costs for ancillary services, such as X-rays and laboratory services, that Medicare would pay each year. Payments for such services could not exceed 110 percent of the preceding year's expenditure. Previously, only payments for routine services were so restricted. Another change set limits on how much Medicare payments could rise each year for various types of hospitals.

The bill also required employers to offer workers eligible for Medicare comparable coverage under their company health plans. This provision was inspired by

the administration view that Medicare was an "unwarranted subsidy" of private business. The plan would make Medicare a secondary source of health benefits for those sixty-five and older and covered by a company plan. Employees who chose not to join their employer's health plan would continue to receive their primary coverage from Medicare.

Federal government employees also were made eligible for Medicare coverage and were required to pay the 1.3 percent payroll tax for their coverage beginning in January 1983.

Premiums for Medicare supplementary medical insurance (part B) temporarily were boosted from a level covering just under one-fourth of the program's costs to a full 25 percent. Under the new law, the monthly premium for the insurance would rise from $12.20 in 1982 to $13.70 (instead of $13.10) in July 1983, and to $15.30 (instead of $14) in July 1984.

The bill also expanded benefits to cover less expensive forms of care, a move sponsors said would save money over the long run by encouraging reliance on such care. Added were Medicare coverage for hospice care of terminally ill patients and a new payment system to promote the enrollment of Medicare beneficiaries in HMOs.

As requested by the administration, the bill also repealed the professional standards review organization program, substituting peer review of Medicare and Medicaid by physician review boards under contract with HHS.

Congressional critics of the cost-cutting changes warned that reducing federal spending on the programs would simply shift costs onto others—hospitals, state and local governments, private insurers, and the poor and elderly beneficiaries of the programs themselves.

The remaining $1.14 billion was cut from projected Medicaid costs. The states would be allowed to charge beneficiaries nominal fees for medical services and to take such steps as placing liens on the property of institutionalized beneficiaries in order to facilitate the recovery of Medicaid costs after death. Other cost-saving moves were administrative in nature and did not require congressional action.

Also in 1982, there appeared to be a gradual shift among state Medicaid programs from short-term cost containment strategies to longer-term structural reforms. Cost-control schemes for Medicaid included setting up agencies to review hospital budgets and rates as well as plans to regulate hospital reimbursements before the costs were incurred (prospective payment plans). Six states (Connecticut, Maryland, Massachusetts, New Jersey, New York, and Washington) had introduced prospective payment plans in 1976 or earlier. According to IHPP, more than two-thirds of the states sought federal approval in 1982 to direct Medicaid recipients to more cost effective health-care systems.

Forecast of Bankruptcy

The Congressional Budget Office (CBO) estimated in February 1983 that the HI trust fund, which financed hospitalization of Medicare beneficiaries, would run out of money as early as 1987. Faced with such a dire forecast, Congress moved with exceptional speed to adopt a radical change in the way the Medicare program bought hospital care for elderly and disabled Americans.

The basic problem, CBO said, was that the cost of hospital care was rising faster than the federal taxes that replenished the fund. Health experts blamed health care cost increases on a number of factors, including simple price inflation and the aging of the population. But many thought the most important cause of rising health costs was the ever-increasing number and sophistication of treatments—surgical and medi-

cal—that ailing Americans, including Mediare beneficiaries, were receiving. In 1982 the cost of health care rose by 11 percent, nearly three times the 3.9 percent general increase in consumer prices for the year.

To hasten its approval, the new "payment-by-diagnosis" Medicare scheme was attached to major Social Security reform legislation (PL 98-21). The law authorized a largely untested new method of calculating Medicare payments to hospitals. When Congress acted, the program was paying—within certain limits—what each hospital said it cost to treat Medicare patients. The new method instead used hospital medical and financial data to assign an average cost, or price, for treating each of 467 "diagnosis-related groups" (DRGs). Under the new plan, hospitals would receive a set rate for a Medicare patient's hospital stay based on that patient's diagnosis. If it cost the hospital less than the payment to treat the patient, the hospital could pocket the difference, but if it cost more, the hospital would have to swallow the excess itself. The central idea behind this new "prospective" is that it would encourage hospitals to budget their resources more effectively.

The Medicare payment reform did not, in itself, end the threat of bankruptcy. While establishing the new method, Congress still did not speak directly to the central question: How much should the nation pay for medical care of its elderly and disabled citizens who were the beneficiaries of Medicare? The new payment plan was expected to give hospitals time and incentives to improve their management before Congress overhauled the entire program.

Skeptics warned that the new system could create powerful financial incentives for hospitals to withhold needed medical treatment from patients, or to extract more money from Medicare by deceptive billing or unnecessary hospitalization.

Health Policy Project (IHPP), a university health-research project funded by the Health Care Financing Administration, forty states applied for waivers between October 1981 and May 1983. Meanwhile, more than thirty states cut back on types of benefits, eligibility groups, and payments under Medicaid in 1981, according to the IHPP.

Additional savings would come from increases in the deductible payments required of Medicare beneficiaries for both the basic (part A) and supplementary (part B) insurance programs, and from other limits on reimbursements.

A Second Round of Cuts

Congress made a number of further changes in Medicare and Medicaid in the Tax Equity and Fiscal Responsibility Act of 1982 (PL 97-248)—President Reagan's tax increase measure—in an effort to reduce federal outlays for health programs in fiscal 1983-1985. The changes would cut spending for the programs by an estimated $14.4 billion over the three years, nearly two and one-half times the amount pruned from the programs in 1981.

The bulk of the spending reductions made by the 1982 act came in Medicare ($13.3 billion). The principal cost-cutting measures revised limits on payments to hospitals and doctors. One provision imposed new caps on the percentage of costs for ancillary services, such as X-rays and laboratory services, that Medicare would pay each year. Payments for such services could not exceed 110 percent of the preceding year's expenditure. Previously, only payments for routine services were so restricted. Another change set limits on how much Medicare payments could rise each year for various types of hospitals.

The bill also required employers to offer workers eligible for Medicare comparable coverage under their company health plans. This provision was inspired by the administration view that Medicare was an "unwarranted subsidy" of private business. The plan would make Medicare a secondary source of health benefits for those sixty-five and older and covered by a company plan. Employees who chose not to join their employer's health plan would continue to receive their primary coverage from Medicare.

Federal government employees also were made eligible for Medicare coverage and were required to pay the 1.3 percent payroll tax for their coverage beginning in January 1983.

Premiums for Medicare supplementary medical insurance (part B) temporarily were boosted from a level covering just under one-fourth of the program's costs to a full 25 percent. Under the new law, the monthly premium for the insurance would rise from $12.20 in 1982 to $13.70 (instead of $13.10) in July 1983, and to $15.30 (instead of $14) in July 1984.

The bill also expanded benefits to cover less expensive forms of care, a move sponsors said would save money over the long run by encouraging reliance on such care. Added were Medicare coverage for hospice care of terminally ill patients and a new payment system to promote the enrollment of Medicare beneficiaries in HMOs.

As requested by the administration, the bill also repealed the professional standards review organization program, substituting peer review of Medicare and Medicaid by physician review boards under contract with HHS.

Congressional critics of the cost-cutting changes warned that reducing federal spending on the programs would simply shift costs onto others—hospitals, state and local governments, private insurers, and the poor and elderly beneficiaries of the programs themselves.

The remaining $1.14 billion was cut from projected Medicaid costs. The states would be allowed to charge beneficiaries

Gross National Product and National Health Expenditures, Selected Years, 1929-1986

Year	Gross national product (in billions)	National health expenditures		
		Amount (in billions)	Percentage of gross national product	Amount per capita
1929	$ 103.9	$ 3.6	3.5	$ 29
1935	72.8	2.9	4.0	23
1940	100.4	4.0	4.0	29
1950	288.3	12.7	4.4	80
1955	405.9	17.7	4.4	101
1960	515.3	26.9	5.2	142
1965	705.1	41.9	5.9	205
1966	772.0	46.3	6.0.	224
1967	816.4	51.5	6.3	247
1968	892.6	58.2	6.5	276
1969	963.9	65.6	6.8	309
1970	1,015.5	75.0	7.4	349
1971	1,102.7	83.5	7.6	384
1972	1,212.8	94.0	7.7	428
1973	1,359.3	103.4	7.6	467
1974	1,472.8	116.1	7.9	521
1975	1,598.4	132.7	8.3	590
1976	1,782.8	150.8	8.5	665
1977	1,990.5	169.9	8.5	743
1978	2,249.7	189.7	8.4	822
1979	2,508.2	214.7	8.6	921
1980	2,731.9	248.1	9.1	1,054
1981	3,052.6	287.0	9.4	1,207
1982	3,166.0	323.6	10.2	1,348
1983	3,405.7	357.2	10.5	1,473
1984	3,765.0	391.1	10.4	1,597
1985	3,998.1	422.6	10.6	1,710
1986	4,206.1	458.2	10.9	1,837

Source: Health Care Financing Administration.
Note: These data, compiled by the Health Care Financing Administration, reflect Bureau of Economic Analysis, Department of Commerce, revisions to the gross national product as of December 1986 and Social Security Administration revisions to the population as of April 1986.

The plan provided that the premium could be increased as medical costs rose. A higher premium was also levied on those persons who delayed enrollment until after the first period when enrollment was open to them and for persons who reenrolled after dropping out.

The secretary of HEW would contract with private carriers to perform major administrative functions of the plan, such as determining rates of payments and disbursing funds.

Medicaid

The medical provisions for the needy already covered under the Social Security Act were combined in a new title (XIX) to the act, which became known as Medicaid. The plan also extended the Medical Assistance for the Aged (MAA) program for the indigent aged to needy persons under the dependent children, blind, and permanently and totally disabled programs; and made eligible for medical aid needy children who did not qualify for public assistance (if the state so provided). Existing provisions of the act covering medical assistance programs would terminate upon adoption of the new program.

States participating in the program were required to provide inpatient and out-patient hospital services, laboratory and X-ray services, skilled nursing home services, and physicians' services. States could provide additional benefits. Needy persons receiving state aid were to be provided with assistance to meet the deductible amounts imposed by the federal basic health plan.

The plan increased the federal share under the existing MAA federal-state matching program so that states with average per capita incomes would receive 55 percent (instead of the existing 50 percent) and states with very low per capita incomes could receive up to 83 percent (instead of 80 percent).

The federal government was required to pick up a 75 percent share of the cost of training professional medical personnel participating in the programs and 50 percent of the other administrative expenses.

States were required to provide a means test to determine eligibility of the needy elderly for the program. The program would not be based on rigid income standards, which could adversely affect persons of some means but with very large medical bills.

1967-1980 Adjustments

From 1967 to 1980 federal expenditures for health care rose with the expansion of the Medicare and Medicaid programs. Congress expanded both eligibility and the variety of services covered. Almost at the start of the programs, it was realized that they were more costly than planners had envisioned. While the Nixon and Ford administrations were concerned about cost containment, Congress did little to curb

program expenditures.

During the period 1967-1977, national compulsory health insurance remained a controversial issue and an elusive goal. While the Nixon and Carter administrations paid lip service to some form of national health insurance, their actual proposals were more limited, with an emphasis on catastrophic health insurance. Even that goal was not realized until 1988.

However, a number of intermediate developments in health insurance occurred in these years. Specifically, certain benefit extensions in the Medicare and Medicaid programs in the 1970s reflected a new emphasis on preventive medicine and less expensive forms of health care, such as health maintenance organizations (HMOs) and home health services.

New Programs/Physicians' Review

Nixon's 1971 health-insurance proposal had three parts: a national health-insurance standards program designed to fill the gap caused by the failure of many private insurance plans to cover catastrophic illness costs; a federal Family Health Insurance Plan to replace Medicaid; and a proposal to encourage the development of HMOs, which provided prepaid comprehensive health care. Despite extensive hearings in House and Senate committees, Congress did not act on these proposals in 1971 or 1972.

However, major alterations of the Medicare and Medicaid program were included in legislation enacted in 1972 (PL 92-603) revising the Social Security Act. The main provisions of that law extended Medicare eligibility to an additional 1.7 million disabled Social Security beneficiaries; provided federal funding for Medicare beneficiaries to enroll in HMOs that provided federally approved services; brought the services of chiropractors under Medicare; provided coverage under Medicare for most Americans afflicted with chronic kidney disease; and established professional standards review organizations (PSROs)—representing local practicing physicians—to oversee Medicaid and Medicare services.

During the Ninety-third Congress (1973-1975), several measures were enacted that coordinated Medicaid eligibility requirements with the federal Supplemental Security Income (SSI) program, which provided federal assistance to the needy aged, blind, and disabled. One part of Nixon's 1971 national health-insurance program—federal assistance to HMOs—was passed by Congress in December 1973, in a more limited form than the original proposal.

In 1975 legislation was passed (PL 94-182) that extended the time limit for local medical groups to set up PSROs. That law also provided that prevailing charges for physician services under Medicare could not be lowered. HEW regulations had tied increases in Medicare reimbursement rates to an economic index, and the 1975 measure represented a legislative victory for medical groups.

Management Reforms

Originally, a number of different HEW bureaus and divisions administered the Medicare and Medicaid programs. In 1977 their functions were consolidated and transferred to the Health Care Financing Administration, which was established in March 1977 as part of HEW. (HEW officially went out of existence May 4, 1980, and was replaced by two departments: the Department of Health and Human Services (HHS) and the Department of Education.)

In 1976 and 1977 Congress moved to correct mismanagement in the two programs when it passed legislation (PL 95-142) increasing penalties for fraud and abuse, strengthening the oversight responsibilities of PSROs, and requiring more ownership information from providers. The bill was the result of three years of congressional study that followed disclosure by

federal and state investigators that kickbacks, fraudulent billings, unnecessary medical treatment, and other problems were occurring in the federal health programs. (Congress in 1976 also established an Office of Inspector General for HEW (now HHS).)

In 1977 Congress approved legislation (PL 95-210) that extended Medicare and Medicaid reimbursement to services provided by nurse practitioners and physicians' assistants in rural clinics. The measure was designed to encourage the development and utilization of rural health clinics in medically underserved areas. In 1978 legislation was enacted (PL 95-292) that amended the kidney disease program under Medicare to provide incentives for patients to conduct kidney dialysis treatments in the home as an alternative to more costly hospital-based dialysis.

Carter Plan Stymied

Carter had made a comprehensive health-insurance proposal one of his campaign pledges, but his 1979 proposal was limited to a catastrophic health-insurance program. Carter's plan was not approved by Congress due in part to concern about the cost of the plan.

Perhaps more importantly, the White House and its allies—the insurance industry, organized labor, and groups representing the elderly—were out-lobbied. While catastrophic health insurance was one of many priorities for those groups, the AMA and the hospital lobby worked against the plan without distraction.

The following year, however, a number of changes were made in Medicare and Medicaid as a part of the fiscal 1981 budget reconciliation bill (PL 96-499). (The 1974 budget act provided for a "reconciliation" procedure for bringing the overall spending by the federal government into conformity with the spending decisions made by Congress.) The bill expanded coverage of home health services under Medicare and payment for minor surgery or tests done outside hospitals. Existing law ordinarily covered these services only if the patient was hospitalized.

Other changes made by the reconciliation bill were meant to encourage physicians not to charge their elderly patients more than Medicare would pay for certain services, but these provisions were not made mandatory. Under existing law, doctors could, and often did, charge well above what the program considered a "reasonable" fee, and patients had to pay the difference.

Reducing the Government's Role

Ronald Reagan was elected president in 1980 on a pledge to reduce the role of the federal government. As a candidate, he endorsed the concept of health insurance in the event of a catastrophe but flatly rejected a national health-insurance plan. He subscribed to a "free-market" or "competition" health policy based on a theory advocated by Alain C. Enthoven, a Stanford University economist specializing in the study of health care. The idea behind a free-market health plan was that if individuals spent their own health dollars, they would demand and get better and cheaper services. Cost and quality would be largely controlled by market forces, not government regulators.

Reagan's First Two Years

Most changes in the Medicare and Medicaid programs during Reagan's first two years were part of a larger administration effort to cut spending for social programs and to reduce the federal deficit. However, administration officials also sought to create pressure for a future overhaul of health-care financing in the United States. Ultimately, said HHS Secretary Richard S. Schweiker, the administration wanted to "use the marketplace to hold down these costs," instead of relying on spending limits and other regulations imposed by Congress.

Medicaid Cuts/Local Autonomy

Congress agreed to cut federal Medicaid spending in 1981 but rejected a Reagan administration proposal to set a rigid ceiling on federal Medicaid contributions to the states. The Economic Recovery Tax Act of that year (PL 97-35) required reductions in spending for Medicaid (3 percent in fiscal 1982, 4 percent in fiscal 1983, and 4.5 percent in fiscal 1984). Those cuts were expected to reduce federal spending on the programs by $5.8 billion.

The 1981 bill also broadened the independent authority of the states under Medicaid, modifying a provision of the 1965 Act allowing Medicaid recipients to choose their own health-care providers (doctors, hospitals, and skilled-nursing facilities), and giving states the option of restricting physicians and facilities available to recipients in certain cases. States would also be able to arrange for laboratory services or procure medical devices through competitive bidding.

Perhaps the most important provision was one that gave the states the opportunity to waive restrictions on the types of services the federal government would fund through Medicaid reimbursements. Previously, Medicaid insurance for certain treatments or procedures had been restricted to inpatient stays. The Medicaid waivers provided a mechanism by which states could be reimbursed for providing home- and community-based health services to recipients who otherwise would have had to seek more expensive hospital or nursing-home care to qualify for federal payments.

According to the Intergovernmental

Expenditures on Hospital Care, Nursing-Home Care, and Physician Services, Selected Years, 1965-1986

Service and year	Total (in billions)
Hospital care	
1965	$ 14.0
1970	28.0
1975	52.4
1980	101.6
1983	146.8
1984	156.3
1985	167.2
1986	179.6
Nursing-home care	
1965	2.1
1970	4.7
1975	10.1
1980	20.4
1983	29.4
1984	31.7
1985	35.0
1986	38.1
Physician services	
1965	8.5
1970	14.3
1975	24.9
1980	46.8
1983	68.4
1984	75.3
1985	82.8
1986	92.0

Source: Health Care Financing Administration.

Advocates maintained that hospital officials would make hard-nosed management improvements and, eventually, influence doctors to use hospital resources more economically.

Congress had laid the tracks for the Medicare payment change in August 1982, when it passed the Tax Equity and Fiscal Responsibility Act (PL 97-248), which included two stringent new limits on Medicare payment rates for hospitals. Sponsors assumed that the limits, together with the existing system of calculating Medicare payments to hospitals, would be promptly replaced by a new payment method. The tax bill also had ordered HHS to design and send Congress a new "prospective" payment system for Medicare within five months.

In ordering a prospective reimbursement system, Congress was asking for a method that would allow the federal government to determine, in advance, how much the program would pay each year to hospitals for treating Medicare patients. Critics said the existing system, which paid hospitals for their costs after services were rendered, inflated medical costs because its financial incentives fostered the wasteful overuse of treatments and procedures, instead of discouraging use. Critics also claimed that Medicare inflation played a major role in driving up the cost of health care nationally.

The 1982 limits were intended to save the federal government money, but they had clear political impact as well. Hospital groups said the harsh new limits were insensitive to legitimate differences among hospitals in operating costs. The limits made the payment-by-diagnosis plan appear to be a comparatively attractive alternative.

The new plan thus had the support of major segments of the hospital industry, including the American Hospital Association and the Federation of American Hospitals, as well as of the Reagan administration and such key members of Congress as House Ways and Means Committee chairman Dan Rostenkowski, D-Ill., and Senate Finance Committee chairman Robert Dole, R-Kan. Other groups, such as the American Medical Association and the Blue Cross and Blue Shield Associations, were critical of the plan but did not work actively to oppose it.

Fee Freeze and Other Changes

Having imposed new out-of-pocket costs on Medicare beneficiaries and clamped new spending controls on hospitals in previous years, Congress in 1984 ordered a temporary halt to increases in Medicare payment rates for doctors. The freeze would be in effect for fifteen months, from July 1984 to October 1985. The fee freeze and other changes in Medicare were included in a deficit-reduction package (PL 98-369) signed into law July 18, 1984.

The legislation also established a controversial "assignment" program intended to keep doctors from simply passing on cost increases to patients during the freeze. Participation in the program was voluntary, but Congress enacted financial penalties for doctors who stayed out of the program.

In addition, the law limited the rate of increase in Medicare payments to hospitals for fiscal 1985 and 1986. The provision applied both to the limits passed by Congress in 1982 to increase payments to hospitals for overall costs of caring for beneficiaries and to the 1983 system that established flat rates of payment per illness.

Major Changes Enacted in 1986

In back-to-back reconciliation bills for fiscal 1986 and 1987, lawmakers in 1986 made major changes in the Medicare and Medicaid programs as they sought to trim federal payments to physicians and hospitals while limiting the financial squeeze on patients.

Fiscal 1986 Reconciliation Bill

The fiscal 1986 reconciliation measure (PL 99-272) extended through December 31, 1986, the physician-fee freeze and limited to 0.5 percent increases in payments to hospitals.

The freeze on doctors' fees had been in place since July 1, 1984, although total Medicare payments to physicians continued to climb sharply nonetheless—11 percent in fiscal 1985, more than triple the increase in

the Consumer Price Index in that period.

The law also made Medicare coverage mandatory for all state and local government employees hired after April 1, 1986, and voluntary for previously hired workers. Covered employees and their employers had to pay the Medicare portion of the Social Security payroll tax.

An array of initiatives unrelated to deficit reduction also were included. Among them were provisions to penalize hospitals that refused to provide emergency care for the poor and to require states to extend Medicaid coverage to pregnant women in two-parent families in which the principal wage-earner was unemployed.

Also included were provisions requiring employers to extend health insurance coverage to laid-off workers and widowed spouses of employees who had been covered by group health plans.

Fiscal 1987 Reconciliation Bill

The fiscal 1987 reconciliation bill (PL 99-509) allowed a 3.2 percent increase in physicians' fees beginning January 1, 1987, and a 1.15 percent increase in Medicare payments to hospitals.

The measure also put the brakes on annual increases in the "deductible" that Medicare patients had to pay for each hospital stay. The deductible, which had been based on the cost of one day in the hospital, rose from $400 in 1985 to $492 in 1986. Without congressional action, it would have reached $572 in 1987. Instead, Congress capped the deductible at $520 and based future increases on the percentage payment change that hospitals received each year.

The legislation provided one year of Medicare coverage for immunosuppressive drugs needed by organ transplant patients, primarily the recipients of kidney transplants. And it imposed a number of safeguards to ensure that the quality of care received by Medicare patients did not suffer because of cost-cutting incentives created by the 1983 law (PL 98-21) overhauling the Medicare payment system.

Finally, the measure permitted states to extend Medicaid coverage to the disabled, pregnant women, and children up to age five who did not qualify for welfare but had incomes below the poverty line.

Concerns about DRG System

Congress also continued to study the impact of its revolutionary prospective payment system for hospitals. Proponents of the DRG system credited it with significant reductions in the rate of increase in hospital costs, mostly because of drops in the average length of stay.

According to HHS, the average hospital stay for Medicare patients under the new system dropped from 9.3 days in fiscal 1983 to 7.7 days for the first two-thirds of fiscal 1985. The growth in hospital expenses slowed from 15.8 percent in fiscal 1982 to 5.5 percent in fiscal 1985. Some of that drop was due to a general ebbing of inflation, but the DRG system was given much of the credit.

The new system was not an unqualified success, however. Critics charged that hospitals were responding to the DRG system's incentives to cut costs not only by operating more efficiently, but also by scrimping on services and discharging patients "quicker and sicker."

A four-month 1985 investigation by the staff of the Senate Aging Committee found evidence that "seriously ill Medicare patients are inappropriately and prematurely discharged from hospitals." The study found that some patients had been incorrectly told that they were being discharged because Medicare did not allow longer stays—that their "DRG had run out."

However, the Reagan administration and hospital officials insisted there was no proof of a widespread decline in quality of care for the elderly. HHS officials said an important check on substandard care was the federally designated system of peer review organizations. Agency officials vowed to strengthen existing HHS requirements that hospitals notify Medicare patients that they had a right to appeal to the local PRO if they felt they were being discharged too soon.

While the DRG system was intended to discourage wasteful practices, critics said some hospitals were losing money through no fault of their own.

Particularly worrisome to key members of Congress was the claim that hospitals serving large numbers of low-income patients were getting short shrift under the new system. Hospitals said that it cost more to treat the poor because they were often sicker than other patients and also often required supplemental services such as translators and social workers.

Responding to that concern, Congress included provisions in the fiscal 1986 reconciliation measure to boost payments to hospitals serving a "disproportionate share" of poor people.

Members also were concerned that the DRG system indirectly contributed to an apparent decline in hospitals' willingness to provide charity care to patients who lacked health insurance or the resources to pay their own bills. The DRG system made it harder for hospitals to absorb the cost of providing free care by increasing charges to Medicare patients.

The new law also included stiff new penalties for hospitals that refused to provide appropriate emergency room treatment because a patient lacked the ability to pay, a practice known as "patient dumping."

More Cuts and Changes in 1987

As it had throughout the latter years of the Reagan era, Congress in 1987 voted substantial cuts in Medicare while authorizing new spending for Medicaid.

Congress took a familiar approach to controlling Medicare spending: Members voted to hold down payments to hospitals and physicians treating elderly patients, while seeking to minimize the burdens placed on the beneficiaries themselves.

Although such efforts in the past had proved successful in curbing program costs, they had not shielded Medicare beneficiaries from growing out-of-pocket expenses. A General Accounting Office study released April 14, 1987, concluded that without the legislated cutbacks of the 1980s, Medicare costs would have been about $13 billion higher than they actually were between 1981 and 1985. During the same period, however, beneficiaries' out-of-pocket costs for hospital care rose by 49 percent and for physician and other outpatient services, by 31 percent.

Lawmakers also continued their pattern of earlier years in expanding Medicaid eligibility to pregnant women, mothers, and young children in families with low incomes who did not qualify for welfare.

Tough Negotiations

In fashioning the 1987 changes, a united Senate and White House ultimately overpowered a House that was determined to spend more and cut less from Medicare and Medicaid. Indeed, the final agreement surpassed by nearly half a billion dollars the mandate of a November 20, 1987, budget-summit agreement that $2 billion be trimmed from the $80 billion federal Medicare program for the elderly and disabled in fiscal 1988, with another $3.5 billion to be cut in fiscal 1989.

And while no specific target was set for added Medicare spending, the final price tag of about $630 million was far closer to the Senate's original figure of $450 million than to the House's $2.3 billion package.

The five days of closed meetings on the fiscal 1987 reconciliation measure (PL 100-203) laid bare an ever-deepening schism among congressional Democrats. The Medicaid spending fight, in particular, "was really a showdown between the spend-and-spend Democrats led by Waxman against the 'new breed' Democrats led by Bentsen and Mitchell, who said the world is looking at us and we look foolish, because the money isn't there," said one Democratic staffer, referring to Henry A. Waxman, D-Calif., chairman of the House Energy and Commerce Health Subcommittee; Lloyd Bentsen, D-Texas, chairman of the Senate Finance Committee; and George J. Mitchell, D-Maine, chairman of the Senate Finance Subcommittee on Health.

Bentsen himself declared in the midst of negotiations December 20 that "we have to meet the realities of the budget. This represents a whole new day after Black Monday," a reference to the October 19 stock market crash that prompted the summit negotiations.

Many House Democrats, though, felt they were the victims of what one called "a devil's bargain" between the White House and Senate Democrats. And they saw the final bill as a mistake from a policy, as well as political, perspective. "The fact of the matter is, it's horrible," said Rep. Ron Wyden, D-Ore., a conferee from Waxman's panel. By failing to add most of the Medicaid expansions envisioned in the House bill, he said, "we're missing chances to save money in the long-term."

While most of the ill feeling expressed by House Democrats was directed at their counterparts in the Senate, Wyden said the root cause of the problem was President Reagan's 1981 tax cuts. "The history of this conference was dictated in the summer of 1981, when Reagan deliberately created these deficits to put pressure on social programs," Wyden said. By 1987, he said, the need to reduce those deficits not only pitted Democrats against Democrats, "it pits human needs against human needs."

Bearing Health-Care Costs

When Congress established Medicare and Medicaid in 1965 under the Social Security system, it specified that Medicare's HI trust fund remain separate from the Old Age, Survivors and Disability Insurance (OASDI) trust funds—the Social Security funds from which retirement benefits are paid. A House committee report on the Medicare legislation said the HI fund would in no way impinge upon the financial soundness of the Social Security trust funds. The independence of the two systems would be assured through such devices as separate trust funds and a separate statement of the hospital insurance tax on individuals' W-2 income tax forms. Like the payroll tax for the OASDI funds, the hospital insurance tax would be levied upon an adjustable taxable earnings base to keep pace with rising earnings levels. However, in 1983 both the OASDI and HI funds faced bleak financial prospects.

From 1982 to 1995, costs incurred by Medicare recipients were projected to increase by an average of 13.2 percent, while covered earnings taxed for Medicare benefits were projected to rise by an average of only 6.8 percent over the same period.

The inflationary nature of health care has ravaged the federal health-care financing system. While the Consumer Price Index rose 134 percent between 1970 and 1981, health-care costs nationwide rose 284 percent over the same period, according to the Health Care Financing Administration.

In 1981, the national rate of spending for medical services grew by 12.5 percent, compared with an overall inflation rate of 8.9 percent, as measured by the Labor Department. This inflation rate for health-care costs was the highest since the department began tracking those costs in 1935.

While Medicare eased the burden of health costs for many, gaps and restrictions

The 1986 Health Dollar

Where It Went

Hospital care	39¢
Nursing-home care	8¢
Physicians' services	20¢
Other personal health care	21¢
Other health spending	12¢

Where It Came From

Direct patient payment	29¢
Private health insurers and other private third parties	32¢
Federal government	30¢
State and local governments	9¢

in the program meant that beneficiaries would up paying far more out-of-pocket than originally expected. According to the House Select Committee on Aging, out-of-pocket expenses for health care represented 15 percent of the mean income of older Americans in 1984—up from 12 percent in 1977, and about the same as in 1966, the year Medicare went into operation.

Medicare in 1984 paid about 45 percent of the elderly's medical bills. Many beneficiaries bought private insurance policies to guard against some of the costs Medicare would not cover.

If the elderly in the 1980s were paying more than they expected for medical care, so was the federal government. When it was enacted, Medicare was expected to cost $8.8 billion in 1990, according to the Office of Management and Budget. By 1985, it actually cost more than $70 billion.

Medicare and Medicaid costs grew each year by 19 percent from 1973 to 1981, a period in which most other entitlements grew at an annual rate of 14 percent.

Federal health outlays in the fiscal

1983 and 1984 (proposed) federal budgets were the fourth largest expenditures after Social Security and related programs, national defense, and interest on the public debt. Health Care Financing Administration figures showed that national health expenditures increased from $75 billion in 1970 to $458.2 billion in 1986. As a percentage of the nation's gross national product, these costs rose from 7.4 percent in 1970 to 10.9 percent in 1986. Per capita national health expenditures, $349 in 1970, reached $1,837 in 1986.

Third-Party Payment

Most health analysts agree that the Medicare and Medicaid systems, along with private health insurance, have been responsible for much of the skyrocketing costs of health care. Health insurance has encouraged policy holders to make fuller use of health services because they do not pay directly for their medical expenses. Instead, they are shifted to a "third party" (private insurance companies or Medicare and Medicaid). The patient pays indirectly for health-care costs through taxes or insurance premiums.

According to the Health Care Financing Administration, patients paid only 29 cents out of every dollar spent on health care in 1981. The federal government paid 29 cents, private health insurance and other third-party payers paid 29 cents, and state and local governments paid the remaining 13 cents. Because third parties were responsible for 71 percent of medical costs, patients were cushioned from the full impact of rising costs.

Louise Russell, in the Brookings Institution budget report for fiscal 1984, pointed out that this was exactly what third-party payments were designed to do. They put into practice the principle that access to health care should not be based on ability to pay for it.

The particular types of health care the federal government and private insurance companies are willing to cover also have been a factor in making health care more expensive. Medicare, Medicaid, and private insurance plans emphasize reimbursement for hospital costs. With the exception of some new coverage of HMOs and hospice care under Medicare and home and community health services under Medicaid allowed in the 1970s and 1980s, less costly home health care and routine and preventive health services have not been covered by these programs.

"The increase in costs to the individual has created a situation which deters preventative medicine and stimulates the use of more expensive services," said Lawrence Lane, spokesman for the American Association of Retired Persons. The patient, given a choice between being reimbursed for hospital services or having to pay out-of-pocket for home health care, has been forced to choose the more expensive care.

The means by which government and private insurance plans traditionally have reimbursed doctors and hospitals also contributed to the inflationary nature of health-care costs. Until Medicare instituted its DRG system for paying hospitals in 1984, both private and public insurance plans reimbursed health-care providers on a fee-for-service basis for "reasonable costs" incurred in the treatment of beneficiaries. This system, still generally in place for physician services, provides little incentive for controlling costs.

Other Cost Factors

Expensive equipment and procedures, highly trained personnel, spiraling liability insurance premiums, and the growth of the elderly population also have pushed up charges for a broad range of treatments and health services.

Advances in medical technology have entailed the use of sophisticated and expensive X-ray equipment such as the computerized axial tomography (CAT) scanner and complicated surgical procedures such as coronary bypass operations and organ transplants.

The threat of malpractice lawsuits has caused doctors to pass the extra cost of malpractice insurance on to their patients and sometimes to overtreat them—increasing medical care fees—in an effort to protect themselves. Hospital workers' wages were raised substantially when hospitals came under the minimum wage law in 1967.

The proportion of the U.S. population sixty-five and over has increased significantly since the Medicare system was set up in 1965. (This includes the old-old, aged eighty-five and older, who are sicker and require more care.) With the growth of the elderly population came a steady increase in the number of persons eligible for Medicare. A big jump in enrollment occurred in 1973 when disabled persons under sixty-five and those with end-stage kidney disease became eligible for Medicare coverage. According to the Health Care Financing Administration, Medicare enrollees in the United States numbered about 28.9 million as of July 1982: 26.0 million sixty-five and older, and 2.8 million disabled recipients under sixty-five. Between 95 and 98 percent of all Americans sixty-five and older were enrolled in the Medicare program in 1982.

A less-recognized factor in increased Medicare expenditures has been the extent of the care received by the elderly population. According to a 1983 CBO study, the elderly have a higher hospital admission rate and more resources committed to them per hospital stay than other segments of the population. The elderly also require more sophisticated and expensive health-care services, such as organ repair and replacement, rehabilitation aids, surgery, and cancer treatments. A November 1980 *New England Journal of Medicine* article reported that the per capita hospital expenditure for the population sixty-five and older

was three and a half times that for persons under sixty-five.

Individual Costs

Although patients paid only 29 percent of the nation's health-care bill in 1981, many elderly patients still found their out-of-pocket expenses excessive. As health-care costs have soared, Medicare beneficiaries have had to pay greater deductibles, copayments, and monthly premiums for supplementary medical insurance.

Between 1965 and 1988, the hospital insurance deductible increased from $40 to $540 and the annual deductible for supplementary medical insurance rose from $50 to $75.

In 1965, the premium for the monthly supplementary medical insurance paid by enrollees was $3. In January 1988 it rose from $17.90 to $24.80.

Along with the deductibles and copayments a patient must bear under Medicare's basic insurance plan, beneficiaries are responsible for 20 percent of the "reasonable cost" of covered medical services (and any costs over that amount) under supplementary medical insurance. Medicare coverage is not available at all for a number of medical services including routine physical examinations, eyeglasses, hearing aids, and dental care.

Because Medicare covers only part of an individual's medical costs, about two-thirds of all elderly persons have bought "Medigap" (supplementary insurance) policies from private insurance companies to supplement Medicare coverage. Congressional investigations in the late 1970s by the House Select Committee on Aging, chaired by Claude Pepper, D-Fla., disclosed that many Medigap policies included coverage that duplicated Medicare. Investigations into alleged widespread fraud in the Medigap insurance industry led to the enactment of a Medigap voluntary federal certification program in 1980. The new program set federal standards for Medigap policies.

Cost Control Strategies

Most remedies proposed for the problems of health-care costs have included one or both of two basic options for reducing expenditures. Louise Russell has defined these as "cost sharing" and the imposition of "budget limits."

Cost sharing is any method that makes individuals responsible for part or all of the costs of the medical services they receive. The amount an individual pays is linked to the quality and price of medical services provided, either directly through service fees or indirectly through insurance premiums. Cost sharing options are effectively built into Medicare in the form of deductible requirements and copayments for hospital fees as well as supplementary medical insurance premiums for doctors' services.

However, the possibility of reducing medical costs in this way has raised difficult questions: How much should an individual be expected to pay? In what form should payments be made? What effects do cost-sharing schemes have upon access to medical services?

Critics of cost-sharing plans are concerned about their effect on the health of the elderly. A 1983 report of the National Council of Senior Citizens observed that cost sharing may prevent elderly people from receiving necessary medical care or impoverish them when they require hospitalization.

Setting budget limits, as defined by Russell, is a method of placing a limit on the amount paid for a package of medical services by Medicare, Medicaid, or private health-insurance plans. The DRG reimbursement system for Medicare uses a budget-limit approach to cost control, setting charges in advance for medical treatment.

HMOs also provide a budget-limit approach to medical cost containment in that they offer a variety of medical services to members for a fixed annual fee. Like an insurance company, an HMO pays for health care in return for a monthly premium. And like a doctor or hospital, it provides health care to those that enroll in the plan. However, because an HMO both pays for and provides health care, there is strong incentive on the part of HMO personnel to avoid unnecessary costs.

An HMO physician is unlikely to keep a patient in the hospital longer than necessary for adequate treatment. In addition, HMOs offer a preventive approach to health care, because they provide both routine health care and hospitalization.

Although HMOs have been effective in reducing health-care costs in the communities where they exist, they have yet to make a significant impact on the national health-care system. And doubts are still expressed by many that HMOs may too often err against giving needed treatment for economic reasons.

Free-Market Theory

Underlying the free-market theory, upon which the Reagan administration's policies were based, was an assumption that Americans received more health services, and at a higher cost, than they needed. Neither patients nor doctors and hospitals were cost conscious because the full cost of medical care was shielded by private or public health insurance.

In addition, proponents of the theory regarded the method by which doctors and hospitals traditionally had been paid (after providing their services) as a temptation to prescribe more and more treatment.

In support of the theory, they cited the accelerating pace of health-care costs after the enactment of Medicaid and Medicare in 1965. Private health-insurance plans also proliferated during this period. A competitive system, its advocates said, would reverse these trends. Providers and patients would become more interested in controlling expenses to keep rates down.

The free-market plan, however, appeared to ignore another factor in the health-care industry—the rapid growth of investor-owned hospital chains and other profit-making medical services. In 1982 they accounted for a quarter of total U.S. spending on personal health, according to Dr. Arnold S. Relman, editor of the *New England Journal of Medicine.*

As in any business, the goal of those organizations was to foster the use of their services, not to restrict them, Relman said. Prices might decline to encourage consumption, but "the fact remains that they are in business to increase their total sales," he stated.

To create a competitive health-care system, its proponents contended that four major changes—combining budget-limit and cost-sharing features—were needed in the national health-care system:

● The cancellation of regulations, such as health planning, peer review, federal antitrust laws, and minimum standards for prepaid health plans (HMOs), to stimulate the growth of new types of health-care organizations.

● The further encouragement of competing medical plans by the provision of a variety of such plans to workers.

● The conversion of Medicare and Medicaid to a voucher system, allowing recipients to spend a predetermined level of their health dollars where they wish.

● The requirement of more cost sharing on the part of insured patients in private plans and public programs. HHS Secretary Schweiker suggested that Medicare patients might at some point have to pay as much as several thousand dollars a year themselves in deductibles. Individual payments would be made more proportionate to benefits through higher taxes and premiums for generous health-insurance plans and tax-free rebates for less costly coverage.

Catastrophic Costs

President Reagan July 1, 1988, signed into law the largest expansion of the federal Medicare program since its inception in 1965. The bill (HR 2470) sought to shield Medicare beneficiaries from catastrophic hospital and doctors' bills related to acute illnesses, and it instituted the program's first broad coverage of outpatient prescription-drug costs. The bill also expanded health coverage for low-income elderly under Medicaid, the joint state-federal health program for the poor.

In both his 1986 and 1987 State of the Union addresses, Reagan had called for action against the economic ravages faced by families who rolled up catastrophic medical bills. "Next, let us remove a financial specter facing our older Americans—the fear of an illness so expensive that it can result in having to make an intolerable choice between bankruptcy and death," the president said.

The administration offered the debate's first major proposal on catastrophic health care costs in November 1986 when Secretary of Health and Human Services (HHS) Otis R. Bowen released a report suggesting various ways of dealing with the problem. The report, which had been ordered by Reagan, made recommendations for financing catastrophic costs for three groups: elderly who needed lengthy hospitalizations; elderly who required long-term, nonhospital care; and the under-sixty-five population at financial risk when catastrophic illness struck.

The centerpiece of Bowen's plan would have expanded coverage of the federal Medicare program, which provided basic health coverage to more than twenty-eight million Americans aged sixty-five and older as well as three million disabled individuals under age sixty-five in 1987. By adding $4.92 to the monthly premium ($17.90 in 1987) most Medicare recipients paid for optional coverage of physician and other nonhospital costs, beneficiaries would obtain coverage for up to one year of hospital care. At the same time, their annual out-of-pocket expenses for Medicare-covered services would have been limited to $2,000.

Although some senior White House officials opposed Bowen's plan because they felt it would have represented federal usurpation of existing private insurance plans that supplemented Medicare coverage, Reagan officially endorsed the portion of the Bowen proposal concerning Medicare in early 1987, within weeks of the time competing plans were introduced in the House and Senate.

Much of the debate over catastrophic insurance had centered on efforts to change the focus of the benefits from acute hospital and posthospital coverage to coverage of long-term care for chronic conditions outside a hospital. Medicare had traditionally been an acute-care-only program. As such, it provided virtually no coverage for preventive services; outpatient drugs for those with chronic illnesses; dental, eye, and foot care; or for the most catastrophic expense of all, long-term custodial care in a nursing home.

House Committee Action

In the House, the catastrophic health care measure was referred jointly to two committees—Energy and Commerce and Ways and Means. They shared jurisdiction over Medicare. Energy and Commerce had sole jurisdiction over Medicaid.

The Ways and Means Health Subcommittee approved catastrophic care legislation that provided benefits to be financed by charging Medicare beneficiaries higher premiums. The measure also required that Medicare patients who were not poor pay income taxes on a portion of their benefits.

The two-part package was built on legislation (HR 1280, HR 1281) initially cosponsored by Health Subcommittee chairman Fortney H. "Pete" Stark, D-Calif., and Bill Gradison, R-Ohio. The subcommittee rejected the more modest administration proposal (HR 1245) proposed by Bowen.

As it emerged from Ways and Means, the bill would have expanded Medicare coverage by about $5 billion per year and relieved the program's beneficiaries of financial responsibility for long hospital stays by providing unlimited coverage after payment of a single annual deductible ($520 in 1987). Under the bill, the deductible would have risen annually at the same rate as Social Security's cost-of-living adjustment—much slower than the medical inflation rate. The measure also would have

extended existing Medicare coverage for short-term nursing-home and home care and capped the out-of-pocket costs for beneficiaries for Medicare-covered doctor and outpatient services.

These benefits were largely the same as those that emerged from the Health Subcommittee. What was different in the full committee markup was financing.

Under the plan that came from the subcommittee, the new benefits would have been financed by making beneficiaries pay income tax on the subsidized portion of Medicare coverage. The subcommittee plan was abandoned in favor of a two-tier Medicare premium.

The first part would have affected the optional physician and outpatient Medicare coverage, which was known as Part B. Nearly all Medicare beneficiaries, more than 98 percent, took Part B coverage. Under the full committee plan, the Part B monthly premium ($17.90 in 1987) would have increased by $1 in 1990, and by $1.50 in 1991.

In addition, the roughly 40 percent of beneficiaries who had incomes high enough to owe federal income taxes would have been assessed an annual "supplemental premium" to help cover the costs of the new benefits. This premium would be assessed regardless of whether a beneficiary chose Part B coverage, although those who did not choose Part B would not have been eligible for the catastrophic coverage offered under that portion of the program.

Several junior committee members during the markup debate tried to change the focus of the new benefits from acute hospital and posthospital coverage to coverage of long-term care outside a hospital. But Stark and Gradison prevailed when they insisted there was no money to pay for long-term care and that it was better to pass a realistic improvement instead of reaching for an unaffordable solution.

"Let's not ruin the good with the perfect," said Stark repeatedly.

The committee did take some tentative steps toward addressing the nonacute care issues. It approved, for example, an amendment offered by Brian J. Donnelly, D-Mass., to authorize $5 million for research into ways of financing and delivering long-term health care.

The two measures considered by the subcommittee (HR 1280, HR 1281) were merged into a single, clean bill, HR 2470, which was reported by Ways and Means May 22, 1987.

The committee, however, was still tinkering with the legislation at the end of June. After prodding by House Speaker Jim Wright, D-Texas, Ways and Means members June 24 approved an outpatient prescription-drug benefit that it asked the Rules Committee to add to HR 2470.

Groups representing senior citizens had been pushing hard for a prescription-drug benefit since plans for catastrophic-care legislation were first announced. They pointed out that while persons aged sixty-five and older represented only 12 percent of the population, they used 30 percent of all prescription drugs. More than three-fourths of the elderly took prescription drugs, at a cost of about $9 billion per year—more than twice the total for the rest of the population.

Among those behind the push for the prescription drug coverage was Speaker Wright. At a meeting the week of May 4, 1987, with Democratic members of the Ways and Means, Energy and Commerce, and Aging committees, Wright emphasized that adding a drug benefit would help put a Democratic stamp on a catastrophic-care plan that first began as a Reagan administration initiative.

Energy and Commerce

The Energy and Commerce Committee approved its version of HR 2470 on June 17, including a slightly different prescription-drug benefit. The committee reported the bill July 1.

The prescription-drug benefit was one of the more controversial provisions approved by Energy and Commerce during a fractious two-day markup. As approved by the committee, Medicare would have paid the full cost of outpatient prescription drugs after a $500 annual deductible was met. The Ways and Means version set the annual deductible at $600.

The Energy Committee's Subcommittee on Health and the Environment June 9 first approved its version of a catastrophic care bill, which would have expanded Medicare to insure beneficiaries against expenses of more than $1,768 annually resulting from acute medical problems, including extended hospital stays.

Subcommittee chairman Henry A. Waxman, D-Calif., added an amendment to include payment of outpatient drugs. Under his plan, Medicare would pay all the costs of outpatient prescription drugs after a beneficiary met a $400 annual deductible. The change would have helped an estimated 4.5 million Medicare beneficiaries.

Waxman's plan was to be financed by raising the premium for Medicare's optional Part B coverage. Waxman said the new prescription drug coverage "addresses one of the most important problems the elderly have when they look at how a medical catastrophe can become a financial catastrophe."

The Final Form

Wright again stepped in to referee negotiations to reconcile the two versions of the bill, and a final House package emerged June 30. The compromise version would have expanded Medicare to cover all costs of unlimited hospital stays after payment of a single deductible ($520 in 1987). It also limited (to an estimated $1,043 for 1989)

Glossary of Terms Used in Debate . . .

The catastrophic health insurance plan involved a major expansion of Medicare. Below is a brief explanation of Medicare and the expansion, along with a glossary of some of the terms used in the debate:

Catastrophic Health Insurance—While some link "catastrophic" to the severity of an illness, policy makers used the term to refer to the financial cost. Some diseases or maladies—Alzheimer's disease, for example, or a severe car accident requiring a lengthy hospital stay—were catastrophic for anyone, but a broken leg could be catastrophic for someone with a low income and no health insurance. The legislation was aimed at protecting Medicare beneficiaries from these catastrophic costs.

Medicare—This federally funded program helped twenty-nine million elderly and three million disabled Americans pay acute-care health costs in 1988. Medicare is funded from several sources: general revenues; beneficiary-paid premiums, deductibles, and copayments; and the 1.45 percent payroll tax collected with Social Security withholding.

Medicare-Covered Services—Medicare traditionally paid only for illness-related health expenses, not for preventive services. Medicare also did not cover the costs of routine dental care, eyeglasses and hearing aids, and outpatient prescription drugs. Medicare did pay (although restrictions were numerous and many patients failed to qualify) the costs for care in a so-called skilled-nursing facility, but it did not pay for care that was more custodial (for example, feeding or bathing) than medical. Medicaid did pay for custodial nursing-home care, but only after a beneficiary had used up virtually all of his savings and income.

Medicare Part A—Officially known as the Hospital Insurance (HI) program, Part A helped pay the costs of inpatient hospital and skilled-nursing care under Medicare. Anyone aged sixty-five or older who was eligible for Social Security or railroad retirement benefits was automatically eligible for Part A coverage. People under sixty-five who received Social Security disability payments (or railroad retirement disability) were also covered by Part A after a two-year waiting period. Just over 100,000 individuals with end-stage kidney disease also received Part A coverage. Persons aged sixty-five or older who did not otherwise qualify for Part A could purchase coverage. The 1987 premium was $226 per month. Part A was financed primarily by an earmarked portion of the Social Security payroll tax. For 1987, the HI share was 1.45 percent of income up to $43,800 for both employers and employees.

Medicare Part B—Officially the Supplemental Medical Insurance program (SMI), this was the optional portion of Medicare available to anyone over age sixty-five and to

the amount beneficiaries had to pay annually for Medicare-covered services under the optional Part B program, which covers physician and other outpatient services.

The bill increased coverage for outpa-

tient mental health, skilled-nursing facility, home-health, and hospice services. It also created "respite care" benefits to provide relief for those who cared for homebound Medicare beneficiaries, and sought to alter

... over Catastrophic Health Insurance

others covered by Part A. About 98 percent of those eligible elected Part B coverage, which paid 80 percent of covered physician and outpatient charges after a $75 annual deductible in 1988. The 1988 Part B monthly premium was $24.80. Premiums financed 25 percent of the cost of the Part B program. The rest came from general revenues.

Long-term versus Acute Care—Acute care refers to services provided by a hospital or doctor for a specific ailment. Long-term care refers to care provided in a nursing home, the patient's home, or anywhere other than a hospital, generally for a chronic condition from which the patient is not expected to recover quickly. Acute care was covered by Medicare, but there were strict limits on long-term care.

'Medigap' Insurance—More than 72 percent of the elderly purchased additional health insurance to pay costs not covered by Medicare. Those policies meeting certain standards could be marketed as federally certified "Medigap" policies. At an average cost of $300-$400 annually, most Medigap policies paid Medicare-required premiums, copayments, and deductibles, but few covered services, such as long-term care, not covered by Medicare.

Spousal Impoverishment—When a married person was institutionalized, Medicaid covered those costs after the couple "spent down" their income and assets to well below the poverty line. Medicaid rules, however, continued to require that most of the couple's joint income be used to pay for the cost of the institutional care. The spouse remaining at home (often referred to as the community spouse) was allowed to keep only a "personal needs allowance," which averaged about $340 per month, usually too little to meet basic living costs.

Skilled-Nursing Facility—This could be a nursing home or a portion of a hospital specifically dedicated to providing nursing care or rehabilitation services that could be performed only by or under the supervision of licensed nursing personnel. Most nursing homes, however, provided "intermediate," not skilled-nursing, care, and many that did provide skilled care were not certified by Medicare. To qualify for Medicare nursing coverage, the beneficiary also had to have been recently hospitalized for at least three days, and a doctor had to certify that skilled care was required on a daily basis.

Supplemental Premium—Originally, all Medicare beneficiaries paid the same premium, regardless of income. The catastrophic bill, however, imposed an additional annual premium based on income. This supplemental premium would be calculated according to the amount of a beneficiary's federal tax liability. For 1989 the supplemental premium was set at $22.50 per $150 of federal tax liability, up to a cap of $800 per beneficiary.

Medicaid rules that frequently left an individual impoverished when Medicaid picked up the cost of nursing-home care for the individual's spouse.

At the same time, it required states to use savings they would realize when Medicare began picking up costs formerly borne by Medicaid to pay the coinsurance, premiums, and deductibles for those beneficiaries with incomes under the federal poverty line.

To avoid adding to the federal deficit, all additional benefits would be paid for by Medicare beneficiaries, either through increases in the Part B premium or through a "supplemental premium" devised by Ways and Means that would make wealthier beneficiaries pay more than those with lower incomes. In 1988, for example, a single individual with an adjusted gross income of more than $14,166 would have been required to pay an additional $580 for the new coverage.

Administration Objections

The Reagan administration—which put catastrophic-expense legislation on the national agenda in the first place—sought to make clear to both committees its displeasure with the shape of HR 2470.

In a June 15, 1987, letter to both panels, HHS Secretary Bowen warned that "should this legislation reach the president's desk in its current form, other senior advisers and I would be forced to recommend a veto."

Bowen said the bill's provisions "contort the concept the president endorsed: to provide an acute care, catastrophic benefit under Medicare. Instead, it appears that the legislation has become a vehicle for modifications and add-ons to the basic Medicare program."

Citing the prescription drug and respite care provisions, as well as the increased mental health coverage, Bowen said enactment of the bill "will result in a cruel hoax on the intended beneficiaries. These program add-ons, combined with the lower out-of-pocket threshold, result in program cost increases that quickly outpace the bill's financing, greatly jeopardizing the stability of the program's design."

At both committee markups, Republican members warned that the cost of the new benefits, particularly the new drug benefit, could quickly outpace the ability—or desire—of beneficiaries to pay for them.

At the heart of the disputes in both panels were wide disparities in estimates of the cost of the program prepared by the Congressional Budget Office (CBO) and HHS. For the original Ways and Means proposal, CBO pegged the cost for 1989 at about $750 million, while HHS said it would be $6.4 billion. Similarly, HHS said the Energy and Commerce plan approved by the subcommittee would cost $8.9 billion for 1989, while CBO set the figure at $1.2 billion.

Democrats said the HHS figures were artificially high because the department opposed the concept of Medicare paying outpatient prescription-drug costs. Republicans countered that Democrats had negotiated with CBO to "make some discounts" on its figures, as Energy and Commerce member Edward R. Madigan, R-Ill., put it.

In the Ways and Means plan, if the costs of the drug program in 1990 exceeded the CBO outlay estimate by more than $1 billion, the HHS secretary would have been required to recommend changes in the program to bring costs back into line.

Similarly, Energy and Commerce members adopted a Waxman amendment raising the annual drug deductible from $400 to $500 and limiting the increase in the premium that covered the benefit to 20 percent in any given year. If more than a 20 percent increase would be needed to cover the cost of the benefit, the HHS secretary would have been required to raise the deductible enough to keep the premium increase at 20 percent.

Before Energy and Commerce agreed on the Waxman drug benefit, members rejected a Madigan amendment that would have replaced Waxman's plan with one that would have required states to cover the full cost of prescription drugs for elderly Medicare beneficiaries whose incomes were 200 percent or less of the federal poverty level.

Waxman, however, argued that if

states were required to use Medicaid funds to pay for drug coverage for the poor elderly, they would likely do so at the expense of other poor people who would be denied benefits.

House Floor Action

The House July 22 overwhelmingly approved HR 2470, but the 302-127 vote belied a palpable lack of enthusiasm among Democrats and harsh partisan rhetoric from Republicans.

As passed, HR 2470 expanded Medicare to provide greater coverage of hospital, outpatient, and prescription-drug costs. To avoid adding to the federal deficit, the bill also would have increased premiums and imposed what amounted to a surtax on the elderly who had a federal income tax liability.

Many doubted, however, that the additional revenue would cover the cost of the additional benefits. Republicans were much harsher in their criticism. "This bill shows how Congress cannot control its insatiable appetite to spend and spend," said Minority Whip Trent Lott, R-Miss. Democrats said they feared that if cost estimates turned out to be too low and steep premium increases were required, senior citizens would balk, and the federal government would ultimately have to foot the bill.

But most Democrats voted "aye" on the theory that something was better than nothing. "We live in an imperfect world," concluded Charles E. Schumer, D-N.Y. "We're not joyous about this, but we'd be less happy with no result."

Many members—both Republican and Democratic—expressed frustration that the bill did not go further toward solving the problem of catastrophic medical expenses. They were disturbed that the bill lacked provisions to address the problem of long-

term care, by far the leading cause of catastrophic health expenses for the elderly.

"Personally, I believe Congress should have used this legislative opportunity to fashion a truly comprehensive response to the problem of long-term care," said Claude Pepper, D-Fla., who nevertheless characterized the bill as "a meaningful step forward." Sponsors of the bill said long-term care had to be left out because it would be far too costly.

Republicans Offer Alternative

Caught in the uncomfortable position of having had the Democrats steal the spotlight on an issue that began as an administration proposal, Republicans tried to take back the initiative July 20 by offering an alternative (HR 2970).

The plan, offered by Minority Leader Robert H. Michel, R-Ill., would have expanded the federal health insurance program for the elderly and disabled less than HR 2470 would have, but still more than originally proposed by Reagan. The Republican plan was defeated.

Although the Rules Committee permitted Republicans to offer their substitute package on the floor, a number of members complained during debate that the Democratic-controlled committee treated members unfairly by not allowing them to offer individual amendments.

At a July 21 news conference to unveil the substitute, Jerry Lewis, R-Calif., charged that the Democratic bill represented "a giant step in the direction of socializing the entire health care system."

The Republicans argued that the Democratic bill contained no provisions for dealing with the problem of long-term care and predicted the benefits added by the Democrats would be too expensive for many elderly to bear.

Their alternative built upon the framework set out by HHS Secretary Bowen, but it added the home-health and spousal-impoverishment provisions from the Democratic version, and it incorporated a limited prescription-drug benefit for poor elderly individuals originally introduced by Waxman, one of the sponsors of HR 2470.

The Republican substitute also contained a number of provisions to encourage insurers to offer—and beneficiaries to purchase—long-term-care insurance policies, including authorizing the creation of a government-sponsored reinsurance program similar to the Federal National Mortgage Association (Fannie Mae).

Because the plan offered fewer benefits, Republicans said it would be less expensive. By 1992, they said, their plan would cost beneficiaries a total of $468 in premiums, while under HR 2470, individuals with incomes high enough to owe the maximum supplemental premium would have paid an extra $1,303. For those with incomes low enough to owe no taxes, however, an estimated 60 percent of the elderly population, the monthly premium for HR 2470 would actually have been lower than for the Republican substitute by 1992: $31.50 compared with $39.

Debate over AIDS

Republicans also argued that because of the way the prescription-drug benefit in HR 2470 was written, it would saddle the nation's senior citizens with underwriting the costs of expensive drug therapy for those under sixty-five suffering from AIDS (acquired immune deficiency syndrome).

That was because AIDS patients who paid into the Social Security system were eligible for Social Security disability benefits, regardless of age, after a five-month waiting period; and twenty-four months after that, for Medicare. AZT, the only drug approved for the treatment of AIDS, could cost upwards of $1,000 per month.

The potential problem, mentioned dur-

ing debate by a number of Republicans, was driven home by William E. Dannemeyer, R-Calif., and Philip M. Crane, R-Ill., who first raised the issue unsuccessfully during Ways and Means consideration of the drug benefit.

The drug benefit in the Democrats' bill, said Dannemeyer, "is inherently unfair and singles out the elderly to shoulder the burden for an exploding disabled population of AIDS victims. . . . While I recognize that someone must bear the health-care costs of these unfortunate victims, I do not believe that the elderly should be targeted for that role."

Waxman countered that the argument was "a straw man." He said nearly all AIDS patients died within a year of being diagnosed, and thus never qualify for Medicare benefits. He also pointed out that the federal government was rushing the development of less expensive alternatives to AZT, which could well be available before large numbers of AIDS patients lived long enough to qualify for Medicare.

But Republicans were persistent, with Crane pressing a motion to recommit the bill to committee with instructions to "ascertain the extent of the tax burden or additional payments required of senior citizens" resulting from drug payments for AIDS patients. Crane's motion was defeated.

Also defeated was an amendment offered by Andrew Jacobs, Jr., D-Ind., to strike from the bill language encouraging the use of generic substitutes for brand-name prescription drugs. Under HR 2470, pharmacists would have been given incentives to substitute generics unless the doctor indicated in handwriting that a brand-name drug was medically necessary.

Manufacturers of brand-name drugs mounted an intensive lobbying effort that was ultimately unsuccessful, although their clout was such that Jacobs's amendment was the only one other than the Republican substitute that the Rules Committee allowed to be offered on the floor.

Jacobs, whose Indianapolis district was home to Eli Lilly and Co., one of the nation's major brand-name drug manufacturers, succeeded in having the generic-preference language struck from the Ways and Means version of the drug benefit. However, it was included in the Energy and Commerce version and in the compromise bill.

Opponents countered that the generic-drug provision represented one of the few real examples of cost containment in the bill, and cited CBO estimates that striking the language would increase costs by more than $400 million.

Senate Committee Action

On May 5, 1987, Finance Committee chairman Lloyd Bentsen, D-Texas, introduced legislation (S 1127) on catastrophic medical expenses that was cosponsored by all of the Democrats on Finance and five of the committee's nine Republicans, including Minority Leader Robert Dole, Kan. (In contrast to the situation in the House, where jurisdiction over Medicare is shared, in the Senate the Finance Committee maintained sole jurisdiction over the Medicare program.)

The full Senate Finance Committee May 29 unanimously approved the bill, which included benefits similar to those in the House version of catastrophic-coverage legislation.

The overwhelming bipartisan support for the Senate bill represented something of a personal victory for Bentsen, who had been championing a similar catastrophic-care plan since 1984 and had made expanding Medicare coverage a priority since the late 1970s. "We now have a rare opportunity to make needed changes in the Medi-

care program," noted Bentsen in an opening statement at the May 28 markup.

House and Senate Differences

That the House and Senate versions appeared so similar was due in large part to what both House and Senate staffers described as "unprecedented" bipartisan and bicameral cooperation. There were, however, a few key differences in the bills.

Both the House and Senate versions of the bill would have financed a majority of their new benefits through what they called a "supplemental premium" to be collected under the income tax system for the estimated 40 percent of the elderly who had incomes high enough to incur a tax liability.

The program created under Bentsen's bill would be completely optional. Only those who enrolled in Medicare's Part B program, which covered 80 percent of physician and other outpatient services, would be eligible for the new catastrophic coverage.

HR 2470, on the other hand, would have expanded benefits systemwide, but it also required all higher-income beneficiaries, even if they had only Part A (inpatient hospital) coverage, to pay a supplemental premium to finance the catastrophic benefits. HR 2470 coauthor Gradison took to calling that bill's supplemental premium "an income-related mandatory user's fee."

Under the Bentsen bill, both the supplemental and basic premiums would have been deductible as medical expenses for federal income-tax purposes, while under the House bill only the basic Part B premium would have remained deductible.

Because the basic monthly Part B premium under the House version would have risen by only $1 (in 1990) while under the Senate plan it would have increased by $4, the House version was more progressive in its treatment of the low-income elderly. But S 1127 was more progressive than HR 2470 in its determination of the supplemental premium. Under the House bill, a single elderly person with an income of about $19,000 would have been assessed the top supplemental premium of $580. Under the Senate version, that person would have paid a supplemental premium of $108. An individual would have paid a $580 premium under the Senate bill if his income was over $42,200, and would not reach the $800 cap until his income was higher than $52,200.

No Long-term Care

As in the House, a number of members of the Finance Committee were concerned about what was left out of the bill.

"The bill does not cover the cost of long-term care services, prescription drugs or balance-billing by physicians," complained John H. Chafee, R-R.I. (The latter is a reference to doctors who charge more for a service than Medicare will pay. Patients then become liable for the "balance.") "Nor does it address the problems of the low-income elderly individuals who will not reach the cap because they haven't got the money to pay for their health care needs.... My greatest fear as we embark on this journey is that when the bill is passed, we will pat ourselves on the backs and say we have solved one of our country's most troubling health care problems. At the end of this process we will not have even scratched the surface."

Bentsen and Health Subcommittee chairman George J. Mitchell, D-Maine, acknowledged the need to address the long-term care and prescription-drug issues but fended off most efforts to add coverage that would have increased S 1127's total cost, estimated at $3.43 billion for 1989, then projected as the first full year of the program.

When John Heinz, R-Pa., offered an amendment designed to provide coverage for 80 percent of the costs of outpatient

prescription drugs after payment of a $500 annual deductible, Mitchell and Bentsen persuaded him to withdraw it by promising they would work to devise a committee amendment when the bill reached the floor.

Bentsen was also able to persuade former Health Subcommittee chairman Dave Durenberger, R-Minn., not to pursue an amendment to expand Medicare coverage of mental health services, and Chafee to withdraw a plan to increase coverage for sick children whose parents faced catastrophic bills.

The committee approved two substantive amendments that were likely to raise the supplemental premium from $12 to about $13.50 per $150 of tax liability. The first, offered by Donald W. Riegle, Jr., D-Mich., eliminated the three-day prior hospitalization requirement for Medicare coverage of stays in skilled-nursing homes. The repeal of the "three-day rule" was also in the House version. The second, offered by Durenberger, for the first time brought preventive screening services into the purview of the Medicare program. Under the amendment, beneficiaries who had special exams to detect breast and colorectal cancer could count those costs toward the $1,700 out-of-pocket cap.

Senate Floor Action

Although Senate Finance completed work on S 1127 at the end of May, the bill did not reach the Senate floor until October. The measure was delayed by Republican and White House objections to its cost.

But during the early fall of 1987, senators negotiated with White House officials and got them to agree to the Senate version of the catastrophic-costs bill and to a Heinz plan to add prescription-drug benefits for Medicare beneficiaries with high annual drug expenses.

In exchange, Senate negotiators agreed to raise the so-called "catastrophic threshold" from $1,700 per year to $1,850. This was the amount beneficiaries had to pay out-of-pocket for covered hospital and doctor services before Medicare would pay all remaining bills.

Negotiators also agreed to an administration request to index annual Medicare premiums paid by beneficiaries to the yearly increase in the catastrophic's program costs instead of to the slower-rising Consumer Price Index, which measured inflation in the economy as a whole.

By a vote of 86-11, the Senate October 27 finally approved its version of the catastrophic medical costs legislation. The Senate then placed the language of its bill (S 1127) under the House bill number, HR 2470.

Although debate on the measure was punctuated by warnings from conservative Republicans that expanding the nation's second-largest entitlement program would send the wrong signal to the nation's deficit-wary financial community, the bill won easy approval. It was aided by the Reagan administration's last-minute endorsement.

The legislative logjam that had held up Senate consideration of the bill since late July was finally broken the morning of October 27. That was the day Heinz took the floor to announce that administration officials had agreed to support the overall Senate bill, plus the prescription-drug benefit.

After the drug amendment was approved, members practically breezed through another two dozen proposed add-ons, adopting eighteen of them, before completing work on the bill.

Like the bill passed by the House July 22, the Senate version of HR 2470 capped the amount Medicare beneficiaries could be required to pay for Medicare-covered services. Both provided unlimited hospital care after payment of a single annual deductible, and both extended current coverage of nursing-home, hospice, and home-based health care. Through the joint state-federal Medicaid program, both bills also sought to pay an increased share of medical expenses incurred by low-income Medicare beneficiaries.

Both bills also, for the first time, provided Medicare coverage for the cost of outpatient prescription drugs—a key feature sought by senior citizens' groups.

Both Democratic and Republican sponsors were visibly agitated at the accusation that the measure was not, or would not continue to be, self-financing. "We're talking about something that's revenue neutral and very responsible, and we went to great lengths to accomplish that," said Bentsen.

Major Items in Disagreement

Although the House and Senate versions sought to accomplish virtually identical goals, they went about that task in very different ways.

One key distinction was that the Senate version of the program was completely voluntary, since it was tied wholly to the optional Part B program, which paid 80 percent of covered doctors' bills and selected other expenses. Although beneficiaries who did not want to pay the added premium costs could drop Part B coverage under the House plan as well, they would still be liable for at least the portion of the new supplemental premium that financed the enhanced Part A (hospital) benefits.

Similarly, the Senate version set a single cap ($1,850 in 1988) on what beneficiaries had to pay out-of-pocket for all except the prescription-drug aspects of the program, while the House version set separate thresholds for hospital, nursing-home, and Part B expenses.

Details of the drug provisions also differed. First, the House version set the initial annual deductible at $500 while the Senate bill required patients to spend $600 before coverage began. But more significantly, the Senate plan would not cover all types of prescription drugs until 1993, while the House version would be fully operational in 1989.

Another sensitive topic was the indexing of the premiums and deductibles in the new program to keep up with inflation. In both chambers members had to perform delicate balancing acts, keeping the program as affordable to beneficiaries as possible, while ensuring that costs did not outstrip the program's ability to pay for them.

Amendments Adopted

The drug amendment provoked by far the most prolonged debate, with supporters citing the need for such coverage under Medicare while opponents expressed concern about future costs. Members on both sides of the issue said they were hampered by the lack of reliable estimates of how much the program would ultimately cost.

"Having a chronic condition necessitating prescription drugs of a costly nature year in and year out both financially and physically amounts to the same kind of catastrophe that the president originally proposed to address," said Heinz.

But others argued the amendment could cause more catastrophes than it would alleviate. "I am convinced that adding drug benefits to the pending bill is like buying a budgetary ticket on the *Titanic*," said Jesse Helms, R-N.C.

In an effort to control costs of the program in future years, and to win administration support, a number of provisions were added to the amendment, including the imposition of a statutory cap on monthly premiums that could be charged to beneficiaries.

If projections showed that the cap would be exceeded in any year, the secretary of HHS would be authorized to take a number of actions, including raising the annual deductible or lowering reimbursements to drug manufacturers and pharmacists. Thus, said supporters, everyone was given an incentive to keep costs down, since everyone suffered if costs grew too high or too fast.

Members also adopted a series of amendments designed to rectify what sponsors described as an unintended inequity that the bill created for Medicare beneficiaries whose pensions were primarily from sources other than Social Security.

Because Social Security was largely not taxable, and because, as originally written, the new supplemental premium would be calculated on the basis of tax liability, many beneficiaries with non-Social Security pensions would have been required to pay more for the benefits than others with identical incomes.

And about 760,000 retired federal employees who were eligible for Medicare already had catastrophic coverage under the Federal Employees Health Benefits Plan (FEHBP).

To try to address the problem, members first adopted an amendment offered by David Pryor, D-Ark., and Pete V. Domenici, R-N.M., that provided those with non-Social Security pensions an adjustment, for purposes of calculating their supplemental premium, equal to 15 percent of the average Social Security benefit.

Members also adopted an amendment by Ted Stevens, R-Alaska, requiring the FEHBP to reduce premiums charged Medicare-eligible enrollees to reflect the transfer of responsibility for catastrophic benefits to Medicare. In addition, Stevens's proposal required the development of a "medigap" policy within the FEHBP to eliminate duplication of benefits.

Other amendments adopted were:

● By Bob Graham, D-Fla., to permit beneficiaries to count the costs of various preventive services and screenings, including mammograms, examinations for colorectal cancer, influenza and pneumonia vaccines, and screening for glaucoma, toward the overall out-of-pocket cap. As reported by the Finance Committee, only triennial mammograms and annual colorectal exams would have been countable.

● By Barbara A. Mikulski, D-Md., to require states to allow the spouse of a person who was institutionalized at Medicaid expense to keep at least $750 in monthly income and $12,000 in assets. The provision was similar to one in the House version of HR 2470.

● By Lawton Chiles, D-Fla., to authorize the training of senior-citizen volunteers to counsel Medicare beneficiaries about available benefits and assist them in completing paperwork required to collect those benefits.

Conference Committee Action

Despite the surface similarities of the House and Senate versions of the catastrophic costs bill, reconciling the massive measure proved both time-consuming and contentious. The conference officially began March 16, 1988; exhausted but jubilant conferees finally completed their task May 25.

The compromise measure provided that starting January 1, 1989, Medicare would cover an entire year's hospital bills after payment of a $580 deductible. Such coverage diminished after 60 days and stopped entirely after 150 days. Beginning January 1, 1990, the program would pay all covered doctor bills in excess of $1,370, although doctors could still bill patients for more than Medicare would pay. Currently, Medicare pays no more than 80 percent of covered doctors' bills. The $1,370 "cap" would rise or fall each year by the amount

needed to keep constant the percentage of beneficiaries who qualified for 100 percent payment of their bills.

The legislation also expanded Medicare coverage of home-health and nursing-home care—although it did not cover long-term care.

The bill offered new coverage for outpatient prescription drugs and "respite" care to relieve unpaid family members and friends who care for severely disabled Medicare beneficiaries.

All of the added Medicare benefits were to be financed by beneficiaries themselves, through increased monthly premiums and a supplemental premium assessed against the 40 percent with the highest incomes.

The bill also made changes in the joint federal-state Medicaid program, which paid health costs for welfare recipients and limited numbers of other low-income individuals. Because Medicare would be paying for many high-cost illnesses formerly paid for by Medicaid, the bill required states to use their portion of the Medicaid "windfall" to extend services not only to low-income elderly but also to poor women and infants.

Few involved with the bill ever really feared a presidential veto, despite frequent White House objections to various provisions. But some of the last vestiges of doubt were erased May 25, when the compromise measure was officially blessed by HHS Secretary Bowen.

Sealing the Deal

Conferees had been optimistic about finishing work on the measure since May 20, when a subconference reached agreement on the complex and controversial portion of the bill providing broad Medicare coverage for outpatient prescription drugs.

But even after an agreement was reached on drug coverage, several key issues remained unresolved, including overall financing of the program, whether all beneficiaries should be required to pay for the new benefits or if participation should be voluntary, and what to do about the House's proposal for a respite-care benefit, not included in the Senate bill and strongly opposed by the Reagan administration.

In meetings May 24-25, Bentsen, Energy and Commerce chairman John D. Dingell, D-Mich., and Ways and Means chairman Dan Rostenkowski, D-Ill., resolved many, but not all, of the outstanding issues. The chairmen agreed, for instance, to make coverage mandatory, as envisioned by the House, but to move closer to the Senate's financing scheme, which would keep constant each year the percentage of beneficiaries eligible for the new benefits.

Respite-care coverage, however, was left to the full conference to decide—reportedly at the insistence of Dingell, who feared it might otherwise be lost. Bowen made clear early in the deliberations that the administration opposed inclusion of the benefit. "It's not an acute-care issue," he said. "It's a long-term care issue and deserves to be part of that debate."

And while most Senate conferees seemed to agree with Bowen, a small cadre, led by Durenberger and Bill Bradley, D-N.J., pushed hard for its inclusion. "All we're doing in the respite-care provision is preserving the informal care-giving system . . . that saves Medicare and Medicaid a lot of money," said Durenberger.

Bradley offered a Senate proposal that would have limited the benefit by tightening eligibility standards. Stark, however, was unhappy with the proposal, because it would have been financed by raising the out-of-pocket cap, thus reducing the number of people who would qualify for the bill's major new benefit.

But just as Stark, chairman of the Ways and Means Subcommittee on Health, made a counteroffer, Bowen made a startling turnabout. If the conference would accept the Bradley amendment, said Bowen, he was prepared to drop his opposition to a respite-care benefit.

With no further debate, Bradley's proposal was adopted. "That's one hell of a deal," laughed Bentsen.

Although Stark still fretted about the financing, he said later that he "just gave up at that point."

Highlights of Bill

The House June 2 overwhelmingly adopted the conference report on the catastrophic-costs measure. The Senate followed suit June 8, clearing the measure for the president, who signed it into law in a Rose Garden ceremony July 1. Following are the major provisions of HR 2470:

Effective Dates. Generally, new Part A benefits (inpatient hospital treatment, home-health care, and care in a skilled nursing facility) were to begin January 1, 1989; new Part B benefits (doctor bills, other outpatient services), January 1, 1990; and broad outpatient prescription-drug coverage, January 1, 1991. All benefits were to be fully phased in by January 1, 1993.

Financing. Except for provisions aimed specifically at the poorest beneficiaries, the new Medicare benefits were to be financed through increases in the monthly premium that 98 percent already pay for optional Part B coverage ($24.80 per month in 1988) and imposition of a new "supplemental" premium that would be assessed on a sliding scale for the 40 percent of Medicare beneficiaries with incomes high enough to owe $150 or more per year in federal income taxes. Beneficiaries could avoid the flat-premium increase by dropping out of the Part B program, but the supplemental premium would be mandatory for those eligible for Part A benefits.

In 1993, the flat-premium increase for all the new benefits was estimated to run about $10.20 per month, while the supplemental premium was not to exceed $42 per $150 of federal income tax liability, up to a cap of $1,050 per enrollee per year.

Hospital Services. Provided up to 365 days per year of hospital care after payment of a single deductible ($580 in 1989).

Outpatient and Physician Care. Capped at $1,370 liability for Part B participants for Medicare-covered services in 1990. Part B pays 80 percent of covered costs after payment of an annual deductible ($75 in 1989). After the cap is reached, the program was to pay 100 percent of all covered costs, although doctors could still charge more than the Medicare-approved amount. The cap was to be increased annually at a rate designed to hold constant, at about 7 percent, the percentage of beneficiaries qualifying for the 100 percent payments.

Skilled-Nursing Facility. Increased from 100 to 150 days coverage of Medicare-approved stays in skilled-nursing facilities and eliminates the requirement that a patient be hospitalized for three days prior to entering a nursing home. Required patients to pay the equivalent of 20 percent of the average cost of a day's stay for the first eight days.

Coverage of Outpatient Prescription Drugs. Beginning in 1991, Medicare was to pay 50 percent of the cost of most outpatient drugs after payment of a $600 deductible. Medicare's share was set to increase to 60 percent in 1992 and 80 percent in 1993 and thereafter; the deductible was to rise at the rate required to keep constant, at about 16.8 percent, the percentage of beneficiaries who qualify.

In 1990, Medicare was to begin to pay 80 percent of the costs of certain classes of very expensive drugs, primarily intravenous antibiotics, as well as costs for equipment and home-health aides to administer the drugs. Medicare was also required to pay 80 percent of costs for the second year and thereafter of immunosuppressive drugs to prevent rejection of transplanted organs. (Previously, Medicare covered 100 percent of the costs for the first year after organ transplant surgery.)

Home-Health Care. Medicare was to cover home-health care seven days per week for at least thirty-eight days, and more if a physician certifies the need.

Respite Care. The bill provided up to eighty hours per year of paid care to allow a respite for family members and friends who care for severely disabled Medicare beneficiaries. To qualify for the benefit, the Medicare beneficiary was required to exceed either the Part B out-of-pocket cap or the prescription-drug deductible, and had to be unable to perform at least three so-called "activities of daily living," such as eating, dressing, bathing, and going to the bathroom.

Hospice Care. The 210-day limit on coverage for hospice care was eliminated, if a patient was still certified as terminally ill.

Medicaid Changes. By January 1, 1992, states were required to pay all Medicare premiums, deductibles, and copayments (including those for the catastrophic program) for elderly beneficiaries with incomes below the federal poverty threshold. States were required to cover all beneficiaries with incomes below 85 percent of poverty by January 1, 1989, with income thresholds rising by 5 percent per year.

By July 1, 1989, states had to provide Medicaid coverage of prenatal care to pregnant women and health care to babies under age one in families with incomes below 75 percent of the poverty level, regardless of whether they are on welfare. By January 1, 1990, states had to provide the services to all those with incomes below the poverty level.

Spousal Impoverishment. The bill gradually raised the income that may be retained by a person whose spouse's nursing-home costs are being paid by Medicaid. From September 30, 1989, until June 30,

1991, it permitted the spouse at home to keep joint income no less than 122 percent of the federal poverty threshold for a two-person family ($786 per month in 1988). From July 1, 1991, to June 30, 1992, the minimum was to rise to 133 percent of that poverty level, and to 150 percent of that threshold after July 1, 1992. The spouse at home was also permitted to keep at least $12,000 worth of the pair's combined assets, and, at state option, up to $48,000, as well as the couple's house.

Long-term Care

Long-term care refers to care, medical or otherwise, needed by chronically ill or disabled individuals who require assistance in dressing, bathing, feeding themselves, and other tasks of daily living.

Some 70 percent of care for the elderly is provided outside of institutions, at least three-quarters of it by friends or family members, according to the Department of Health and Human Services' 1982 National Long-Term Care Survey.

But it is nursing-home costs, which in 1988 averaged $23,000 per year, that pose the greatest financial jeopardy to a family's economic well-being. Since the need for long-term care rises with age, the "graying of America" is threatening to turn a serious problem into a crisis.

Indeed, a consensus seemed to be emerging on Capitol Hill in the late 1980s that the issue is one that must be addressed sooner rather than later, and that any solution would likely have to involve the government at some level.

"This is one of the major gaps in our health-care system," said Sen. George J. Mitchell, D-Maine, chairman of the Finance Committee's Health Subcommittee.

"I think there's a big clamor out there that people want long-term care covered, and that there's a big role for the government to play," added Rep. Henry A. Wax-man, D-Calif., chairman of the Energy and Commerce Subcommittee on Health and the Environment.

Poll Results

The clamor for long-term care is reflected in a torrent of poll results showing that the public not only wants government support for long-term care but is willing to pay for it through higher taxes.

Among the findings:

• Eighty-five percent of respondents to a poll conducted in July 1987 by the Princeton, N.J.-based RL Associates said it was time to consider some sort of government program for long-term care. More than 70 percent said they would be willing to pay higher income taxes to support the cost of long-term care for the elderly.

• Eighty percent of those polled by Louis Harris and Associates in February 1988 said they favor a federal program to provide long-term home care. Seventy-one percent favored financing such a program by lifting the current $45,000 cap on income subject to the 1.45 percent Medicare payroll tax, and that group included nearly three-fourths of those with incomes over $50,000—the very people who would have to pay more taxes.

• Forty-seven percent of those polled by

Peter D. Hart Research Associates in June 1987 said they would be willing to pay more taxes to reduce the cost of health care for the elderly. By 13 percentage points, this was the most positive response received among the five programs respondents were asked about. The others included programs for early-childhood education and health, aid to farmers, spending on defense, and legislation to lower the federal budget deficit.

● Providing better and more affordable long-term care for the elderly was the top priority of a sampling of Americans between the ages of eighteen and forty-four asked to select from a list of ten issues those most important for President Reagan's successor to address. Long-term care garnered more votes in the poll, conducted by Hart for *Rolling Stone* magazine, than finding a cure for AIDS or cleaning up toxic waste and pollution.

"It's clearly an important issue," said Thomas Riehle, an analyst with Hart's firm. "People of all ages realize it's a real threat to their own financial security."

Leadership, Complexity

To a large extent, the future of the issue will be determined by who occupies the White House in 1989. Without President Reagan taking the lead on the catastrophic-costs issue, congressional observers agreed, that bill might never have been passed.

"This whole issue depends on leadership," said John C. Rother, director of legislation, research, and public policy for the American Association of Retired Persons (AARP).

Even presidential backing, however, will not guarantee quick action on Capitol Hill. The problem of financing long-term care is exceedingly complex, because both the types of care needed and the settings in which care is delivered vary widely.

"We'll never have one bill where we can say, 'If this passes tomorrow, we'll take care of the whole problem,' " said an aide to Sen. Dave Durenberger, Minn., ranking Republican on the Finance Health Subcommittee. Compared with long-term care, "catastrophic is really a tiny, tiny problem that requires a very simple, almost technical solution," she said.

Underwriting long-term care will be not only complicated but costly—too costly, most experts agree, for either the government or those who need the care to pay the entire bill.

For example, the Congressional Budget Office estimated that the measure (HR 3436) promoted by Rep. Claude Pepper, D-Fla., in the One-hundredth Congress to provide long-term home care for all who need it would have cost $4.5 billion in fiscal 1989, rising to $7.6 billion by 1992.

Nursing-home care is even more expensive, costing Americans $38.1 billion in 1986, according to the Health Care Financing Administration. More than half that bill was paid by residents or their families. The state-federal Medicaid program for the poor paid 41.4 percent of the tab, but only after beneficiaries depleted nearly all their life savings. Medicare, which has severely limited coverage of nursing-home care, paid 1.6 percent of the total bill, while private insurance companies covered just under 1 percent.

Long-term-care costs for the elderly are so high that even if spread out over the entire population aged sixty-five and over, they still exceed $1,200 per person per year, Joshua M. Wiener told the House Budget Committee in October 1987. Wiener, a senior fellow with the Brookings Institution in Washington, D.C., is a key analyst of long-term-care financing.

But for all the difficulties, the issue is far more developed than it was before the debate began over the catastrophic-costs bill. "A couple of years ago, most members of Congress didn't realize Medicare didn't pay" for long-term care, said Waxman.

And while private insurance for long-term care is still in its infancy, covering only about 500,000 of the nation's thirty-two million Medicare beneficiaries, "that private-sector involvement is tacit recognition that it's solvable," said Wiener. "The private sector deserves credit for changing the scope of the debate."

Pepper's Proposal

The legislative focus in the long-term-care debate in the One-hundredth Congress was HR 3436. The so-called "Pepper bill" would have the federal government pay for at-home long-term care at an estimated cost of $30 billion over five years. The benefit would be financed by eliminating the cap on income subject to the 1.45 percent Medicare tax paid by workers and their employers. Currently, the tax is assessed against the first $45,000 of income per year.

The House June 8, 1988, rebuffed the proposal, but its action proved no real test of congressional enthusiasm for either the issue or its principal champion.

"Today's action marks the beginning, not the end, of the debate over the best way to meet the need for long-term care," said Dan Rostenkowski, D-Ill., shortly after the House by 169-243 defeated a rule (H Res 466) that would have allowed debate of HR 3436. The House action effectively killed the bill.

Rostenkowski, chairman of the Ways and Means Committee, noted that he expected Rules Committee chairman Pepper to serve on a long-term-care commission created as part of legislation (HR 2470) cleared by the Senate the same day to protect Medicare beneficiaries from catastrophic costs of acute illnesses.

The commission would report back within six months, and, said Rostenkowski, "I look forward to reviewing those recommendations with Chairman Pepper and our new president."

"It was certainly not a wasted effort," said Ed Howard of Villers Advocacy Associates, a key organizational backer of the measure. Pepper, he said, "has placed this issue squarely on the agenda of things the 101st Congress *must* deal with."

Added Bruce Fried, executive director of the 140-organization National Health Care Campaign: "We lost the bill, but an issue was born."

Finding a Vehicle

Representative Pepper had been dissatisfied with the limited scope of the catastrophic-costs bill (HR 2470) ever since it was outlined in February 1987 by Fortney H. "Pete" Stark, D-Calif., and Bill Gradison, R-Ohio, chairman and ranking minority member, respectively, of the Ways and Means Subcommittee on Health.

On March 2, 1987, major groups representing the elderly, including the twenty-eight-million-member American Association of Retired Persons and the National Council of Senior Citizens, held a press conference to complain that the bill did not address the issue of long-term care, which they consider the principal health-related catastrophe threatening the financial well-being of senior citizens. The press conference—pointedly conducted in the House Rules Committee chamber—featured Pepper sitting under a leaky umbrella to illustrate the catastrophic bill's "holes."

Many of those holes were ultimately filled as HR 2470 threaded its way through the legislative process. But the tremendous cost of long-term care kept sponsors from attempting more than the most modest provisions to help those with chronic rather than acute health problems.

Those provisions did not please Pepper.

'Long Term Care '88' Campaigns . . .

It is a sophisticated national campaign complete with flashy brochures and an extensive grass-roots organization. It employs pollsters to track voter support and professionals to capitalize on paid and free media. And it focused most of its early efforts on events and voters in Iowa and New Hampshire.

But this campaign has no candidate. Long Term Care '88 is devoted not to the election of a particular person, but instead to the coronation of an issue. A consortium of more than one hundred health, welfare, senior citizens', and labor organizations, LTC '88 seeks "to place the issue of long-term care squarely on the national agenda by encouraging candidates to say how they will protect American families from the crushing financial burden of long-term care."

Key backers of the campaign include the twenty-eight-million-member American Association of Retired Persons (AARP) and the Villers Foundation, an organization devoted to the "empowerment" of the elderly, particularly those with low incomes.

"Our goal is on Jan. 20, 1989, to have a president ready to mention long-term care in his Inaugural Address, a populace ready to support it and policy makers with some idea of what to do," said Villers's Ronald F. Pollack.

LTC '88 has gone to great lengths to emphasize that long-term care is a problem for entire families, rather than a concern of the elderly alone. The group's literature highlights the stresses on middle-aged adults who must care simultaneously for aging parents and their own children, and the plight of citizens of all ages who require care as a result of accidents or chronic disease.

Still, organizers are sensitive to charges that attention to long-term care may come at the expense of other family programs, particularly those aimed at low-income children. "Children's health and related concerns *should* be of utmost priority," said Pollack. "The political difficulty with achieving that agenda is that those issues require

On June 24, 1987, Pepper and Aging Committee chairman Edward R. Roybal, D-Calif., introduced their long-term care plan (HR 2762). In July Pepper held up consideration of the catastrophic-costs bill by threatening to attach his bill to it when HR 2470 came before the Rules Committee. Sponsors of HR 2470, several of whom said they were sympathetic to Pepper's proposal, fought to keep the plan off the catastrophic bill, fearing the controversial financing would jeopardize the package. They also were afraid of a presidential veto, as Reagan at that point already had serious reservations about the catastrophic-costs bill.

At a "summit" lunch July 9, House Speaker Jim Wright, D-Texas, was able to persuade Pepper not to add the long-term-care bill to HR 2470. In exchange, Wright promised that Pepper would have a chance for an up-or-down House vote on his plan "on an appropriate vehicle."

On October 15, 1987, the House Education and Labor Committee approved HR 3436, making technical corrections to the Older Americans Act reauthorization. At the brief markup, Education and Labor Committee chairman Augustus F. Hawkins, D-Calif., announced that the bill was merely a shell that Pepper could fill with

... to Put Issue on National Agenda

middle-class altruism. Long-term care is more powerful politically, because it combines altruism with self-interest."

The campaign focused its early efforts (and some $1 million in cash and in-kind services) on the 1988 presidential race. In that way, LTC '88 was able to reach several important audiences at once, organizers said. While educating voters and the candidates about the issue, LTC '88 at the same time managed to play off the national media trailing after those who would be president.

In Iowa, for example, LTC '88 recruited Sens. Tom Harkin, D, and Charles E. Grassley, R, to quiz all the presidential hopefuls from their respective parties about their views on long-term care. All the candidates were asked the same questions, including whether they would mention the issue in their inaugural address (all said they would). LTC '88 then bought television air-time to show five-minute versions of each of the interviews, which ran throughout January 1988.

The candidates were prepared for the Iowa interviews because a month earlier, all except Democrat Gary Hart and Vice President George Bush participated in individualized long-term care forums sponsored by the Villers Foundation and a local radio and television station. At each forum, candidate and audience were shown a tear-jerking seventeen-minute video called "Our Parents, Our Children, Ourselves," commissioned by LTC '88 to outline the problem, after which the candidate could make a brief presentation and then field questions.

And while the audience for the forums was limited, the exposure they prompted was not. In December, only days after his forum in New Hampshire, Sen. Robert Dole, R-Kan., was tapped in a nationally televised debate to ask the first question on domestic issues of fellow candidate Pat Robertson. His question: What would Robertson do about the problem of long-term care?

---

the text of his home-care bill.

"Let the chair state that the purpose of the bill before you is primarily to give [Representative] Pepper an opportunity to facilitate the movement of a bill of his: the Medicare Long-Term Home-Care Catastrophic Protection Act," Hawkins said. "The proposal is merely a vehicle."

Hawkins pointed out the Pepper "has been very cooperative with the committee, and I have simply offered this as an opportunity to give him a break in order to try to accomplish a legislative purpose of his." Committee Republicans seemed perfectly willing to go along.

Bypassing Ways and Means

In November 1987, Pepper persuaded his Rules Committee to pave the way for a 1988 floor vote on his long-term care bill, without sending the measure through Ways and Means or any other standing committee.

He was heatedly challenged by Ways and Means Committee chairman Rostenkowski. The Pepper-Rostenkowski debate featured two masters of the art. "There was a sense of drama you don't get very often," said one staffer.

Rostenkowski, accompanied by Ways

and Means Health Subcommittee chairman Fortney H. "Pete" Stark, D-Calif., based his case against the bill on both procedural and substantive grounds.

Jurisdictionally, he argued, consideration of the bill on the House floor "would be tantamount to discharging Ways and Means" from its normal duty to consider measures involving taxes. That, he said, would constitute "a serious violation of House procedures" and "establish a precedent I do not see how any committee of the House could support."

Rostenkowski and Stark also argued that Pepper's bill was substantively flawed. Fewer than half the number of home-health agencies needed to furnish the care envisioned under the measure existed, Rostenkowski said. Stark pointed out that as drafted, the bill would permit any two-year-old child to qualify for the benefits by virtue of being unable to dress, eat, walk, or go to the bathroom without assistance.

But Pepper brushed off their complaints. "I realize it is an extraordinary procedure," he said of his desire to bypass the normal committee review, "but this is an unusual situation we have." He reminded members of the Speaker's promise of a vote on his bill.

Pepper dismissed the substantive complaints as well. "The American people have declared themselves that the greatest need there is in the medical field is for long-term care," he said. He cited a poll conducted for the Long Term Care '88 campaign showing that six of seven respondents felt it was time to consider some government program for long-term care and that, by a 5-to-2 margin, respondents said they were willing to see taxes increased to pay for such a program.

Rostenkowski remained unconvinced. "It's not easy to come up and be against something that's quite acceptable to the American public," he said. "It's not easy being the chairman of a committee where the bottom line is how much does it cost and

can we afford it. But sometimes you can't be as generous as we want to be. You know Christmas season is over as far as the Congress of the United States [is concerned]."

Fired back Pepper: "You take the loftier, statesmanlike view, 'Well, let's wait awhile about this matter. We'll get around to it in time.' I realize you see the broader view. I just can't help thinking about those individual people."

Pepper also argued that time was of the essence because the Senate Finance Committee, as part of its budget-reconciliation package, had already appropriated his financing by recommending that the wage cap on the Medicare tax be lifted to pay for deficit reduction. (The proposal was ultimately eliminated in conference.)

The Finance Committee, he said, "has already grabbed hold of that money as best they can.... If we don't ask now, this money may be used for general purposes. I am saying the best thing we can do is to give it to the people who have a long-term chronic illness, and help them and their families survive without being ruined."

Pepper tried to mend fences with members of the committees that would be bypassed by his unusual maneuver. "We want to make it clear we want the House to have the widest possible opportunity to improve the bill on the floor," he said.

At the November 17 Rules Committee meeting, Pepper also declared, "This is a chance within the near future to get the American people something they've been praying for. I hope you understand how deeply I feel about this."

In the end, Pepper—with his home-field advantage—prevailed, persuading his committee to grant a rule allowing a vote on HR 3436, which carried an amendment substituting Pepper's long-term care bill (HR 2762) for its original text.

"When you own the umpire, chances are you're going to win the ball game," growled Rostenkowski before the votes were tallied. Rostenkowski vowed to take his fight against the bill to the more neutral turf of the House floor.

Debate Continued

The House leadership announced even before an agreement on HR 2470 was reached that Pepper would have his vote the week following final approval of the catastrophic-costs bill.

On the support side, Pepper had plenty of company. His original bill had more than 150 cosponsors, including such strange bedfellows as House majority whip Tony Coelho, D-Calif., and conservatives Henry J. Hyde, R-Ill., and Christopher H. Smith, R-N.J.

The bill also enjoyed the active support of more than ninety health, children's, senior citizens', and social-service organizations. The National Health Care Campaign, a consortium of some 140 such organizations, declared May 2, 1988, "Pepper Day," and orchestrated the delivery by senior citizens of small bags of green peppers to every congressional office as a mark of support for the bill.

But by far the most effective lobbyist was Pepper himself.

"I think America is wealthy enough to take care of people according to their needs," Pepper told an audience at the National Press Club May 19, 1988, asserting that his bill "will save almost 1 million people a year from becoming destitute."

Pepper also defended the bill's financing, which many called a thinly disguised tax hike. Referring to Chrysler Corp. chairman Lee A. Iacocca, Pepper said, "Mr. Iacocca, who's reputed to make $20 million per year, would pay his 1.45 percent and still have $19,750,000 left. With a little help from food stamps, I think he could get by."

The Press Club audience was amused, but not so a coalition of health-care providers, insurance interests, and business groups.

The coalition, the Coordinating Committee for Long-Term Care Policy, included such organizations as the U.S. Chamber of Commerce, the Health Insurance Association of America, and the American Health Care Association, which represents the nursing-home industry.

In a large display advertisement in the May 26, 1988, edition of the *Washington Post* headlined "Haste Makes Waste," the group charged that "rushing HR 3436 through Congress is the wrong medicine to cure the nation's long-term care problem." The problem, said the ad, could be better addressed by a "cooperative effort of public and private sectors."

At a press briefing, spokesmen for the group said the bill's financing presented a serious equity problem, because only 5 percent of the population (those who earn in excess of $45,000 per year) would be paying for a large new entitlement program.

But the most outspoken opponent of the measure was House Ways and Means chairman Rostenkowski.

"This whole exercise has a lot more to do with politics than policy," Rostenkowski told the Coordinating Committee for Long-Term Care Policy in a speech May 12, charging that the program envisioned in the Pepper bill "throws money at a problem without seriously considering the mechanics of delivering on the bill's promises."

Rostenkowski and others contended that adequate home health services were in short supply or completely unavailable in many parts of the country. They also said that no administrative mechanism existed to determine eligibility for the benefits or to set appropriate payments for providers.

Wrote Rostenkowski in a May 23 "Dear Colleague" letter: "This is an open invitation to unscrupulous individuals to quickly set up low-quality home-service

Members Have Plenty of Praise for Pepper ...

Claude Pepper, with tears in his eyes, could not persuade his House colleagues to pass his long-term care bill, but he did bring them to their feet in a thundering ovation. His voice cracking, the Florida Democrat implored a packed chamber during the climactic moments of the June 8, 1988, debate on the rule for House floor consideration of HR 3436. "I ask you, my colleagues, when you go home tonight and you close your eyes and you sleep and you ask, 'What have I done today to lighten the burden upon those who suffer?' at least you could say, 'I helped a little bit today; I voted to help those who needed help.'"

His backers were characteristically venerating. "This is a dream come true for him to have this become law," said fellow Rules Committee member and chief deputy majority whip David E. Bonior, D-Mich. "Do not disappoint Sen. Pepper today. Stand with Sen. Pepper. Stand with the elderly and vote 'yes.'" (Pepper served in the Senate from 1936 to 1951.)

But even his opponents paid tribute to the eighty-seven-year-old lawmaker. "All of us have enormous respect for Chairman Pepper and his commitment to protecting the economic well-being of the elderly," said Ways and Means chairman Dan Rostenkowski, D-Ill., who led the fight against Pepper's bill. Added another key opponent, John D. Dingell, D-Mich., chairman of the Energy and Commerce Committee, "It is a matter of personal distress of the highest order that I find us on opposite sides." Younger members were equally deferential. "I admire, respect and love my colleague from Florida who introduced this bill," said Jim Slattery, D-Kan., who was among the more vocal opponents of the bill.

Pepper's bill would have provided long-term home health care for all Americans requiring it, regardless of age. Although the long-term care issue was a politically potent one in 1988, and even with Pepper's personal popularity, the bill could not overcome major substantive and jurisdictional obstacles.

On the substantive side, critics worried about creating a massive new entitlement agencies to capture the available federal dollars."

Bringing such a bill to the floor, Rostenkowski said, "raises expectations of the elderly that will not be met, adding to public cynicism about Congress.... For the House to consider a major bill that is probably unpassable and clearly unworkable is not being responsive to the elderly. It is irresponsible and misleading."

He cited a Congressional Budget Office estimate that within the first five years, the cost of the benefits would begin to outstrip revenues, requiring cost-containment measures.

Rostenkowski also made no secret of the fact that he was annoyed to see the regular legislative process short-circuited.

"The committee of jurisdiction has been effectively discharged, without the normal requirements and procedures for such action having been followed," he wrote in the May 23 letter. "I cannot remember a more serious violation of the House rules, and am very concerned about the precedent this will set for all House committees."

... Despite Voting Down His Long-term Care Bill

program, about whether cost estimates (nearly $30 billion over five years) were too low, and about whether the bill actually promised care it could not deliver, given the current shortage of the sort of health professionals who would be needed to provide the services.

And on the jurisdictional front, the bill's unusual route to the floor sidestepped committees headed by Dingell and Rostenkowski, who, a June 1988 *Washington Post* article noted, "when crossed . . . can exhibit some of the less amiable personality traits of the grizzly bear."

But what made the 'no' vote so painful for many was not merely that Pepper is revered by the nation's senior citizens, nor that, as chairman of the Rules Committee, he is one of the more powerful members of the body. What made it so difficult was that so many Democrats owed him so much.

One prominent Democrat, who called his "no" vote the hardest he had cast in recent memory, said that "Claude Pepper has been the Ronald Reagan of this party for eight years. He'd come to your district and draw 2,500 or 3,000 people. Rostenkowski couldn't do that."

Indeed, in 1982, Pepper was one of the most sought-after campaigners in the House. Traveling alone and carrying his own bags, he made public appearances for seventy Democratic candidates in twenty-five states. "There's probably 30 people who wouldn't even be here if it wasn't for him," said the member.

Pepper is not unaware of his impact. At a press conference the day before the House vote, he warned that "a lot of Republicans are going to get defeated if they vote against this bill." And after a vote in which a considerable portion of Democrats deserted him, he said, "99 Democrats forgot about what the Democratic Party stands for." Those members, he hinted, may wait a long time for him to visit their districts. "I'm not going to have very much enthusiasm to support those who voted against me," he said. "The ones I support will have to be the ones who believe, as I do, in liberal, compassionate causes."

Pepper rejected that argument, noting that Ways and Means had almost a year in which to hold hearings and develop its own proposal. When Rostenkowski ignored the opportunity, the Pepper-led Rules Committee June 2 struck from the rule governing floor debate on HR 3436 language providing for a Ways and Means amendment.

And while the House Democratic leadership took no position on the bill, Rostenkowski's complaints about the process seemed to touch a nerve. "Nobody's jurisdictional toes have been stepped on,"

snapped Wright during a May 2 lunch with reporters. "Mr. Pepper had every legal right to propose his program as amendatory" to HR 2470, Wright said, and when he agreed not to, "I told him we would give him a separate opportunity to have that bill considered in its own right. . . . Members of the committees of jurisdiction were present when the promise was made, and they were relieved" that Pepper was not going to seek to attach the proposal to the catastrophic-costs measure.

The dispute took on a personal tone at

times. Several people who were present during the May 12 Rostenkowski speech to the Coordinating Committee for Long-Term Care Policy reported that the Ways and Means chairman imitated the shuffling walk of the eighty-seven-year-old Pepper and said he feared his colleagues would vote for the bill because the Florida Democrat is "a nice old man."

Some groups representing the elderly felt caught in the middle on the Pepper bill. They strongly supported a federal program to help pay for long-term care, but officials for some of the groups privately had reservations about the workability of Pepper's plan. And they were unhappy about opposing Rostenkowski, not only because he helped win passage of HR 2470, the largest expansion of Medicare in the program's history, but also because he would remain a crucial player on future health-care bills.

Vote on Rule

On June 8, 99 Democrats joined 144 Republicans in defeating the rule to allow the long-term-care bill to come to the House floor, while 145 Democrats and 24 Republicans supported Pepper. Most attributed the outcome to the combined efforts of Rostenkowski and Energy and Commerce chairman John D. Dingell, D-Mich., two of the most powerful committee chairmen in the House.

The two, whose panels were bypassed by Pepper as he sought to win a floor vote on his bill, were frequent rivals and not particularly friendly toward one another. But with turf at stake, they teamed up in the week leading up to the vote. They barraged members with "Dear Colleague" letters, personal notes, and phone calls in a successful bid to persuade those who would need their favors in the future to see the issue their way.

"They're not gods, but they put an awful lot of heat on members," said a

visibly deflated Pepper during a news conference after the vote. "Some members called me this morning and said, 'Claude, I was going to vote with you, but the chairman's called me three times already this morning.'"

One thing the vote was not, members insisted, was a rejection of the wishes of the nation's elderly, a powerful lobby increasingly portrayed by the media as "pushy."

"We need long-term care," said one Democratic member who voted against the rule. "Regrettably, this wasn't the bill."

Others noted that the most influential senior citizens' organization, the American Association of Retired Persons, while officially supporting the bill, took no position on the vote on the rule—a clear indication the organization would not seek electoral retribution against those who voted 'no.'

"AARP sat it out," said Ed Howard of Villers Advocacy Associates, a group that supported the bill. "When the largest and most powerful elderly group doesn't even take a position, how can you say it was definitively a defeat for the elderly?"

Some members, including Majority Leader Thomas S. Foley, D-Wash., seemed genuinely troubled by the unorthodox procedure that put the bill on the House schedule in the first place without sending it first through the committees with jurisdiction over health legislation.

Although defeat of the rule precluded full debate of the measure, members also had serious substantive objections to the measure, particularly its cost. Still, the vote remained a very difficult one for many members, particularly Democrats.

"On one side, you had two powerful chairmen whose paths you're going to cross over and over again if you're planning to be around here a long time," said one Democrat. Undecided until literally the last minute of the vote, he finally opted to support the rule "because long-term care is an issue that's been important to me since I came to Washington. I'd want to structure the bill more carefully, but I didn't want to say 'no.' "

Another wavering Democrat came to the opposite conclusion. "Congress ought to be on notice that the American public is ready for long-term care," he said, "but in the end, the substantive problems were so overwhelming you just couldn't buy into it."

Senate Measures

By the end of August 1988, the Senate had taken no action on a companion bill (S 1616) to Pepper's measure. The bill was sponsored by Paul Simon, D-Ill.

Hearings were held in mid-1988 on another long-term-care measure, S 2305, which was introduced by Senate Finance Subcommittee on Health chairman Mitchell. His bipartisan group of cosponsors included fellow subcommittee members John H. Chafee, R-R.I.; John Heinz, R-Pa.; and John D. Rockefeller IV, D-W.Va. While a host of bills on long-term care had been introduced in the One-hundredth Congress, Mitchell's was the first from a leader of one of the committees with jurisdiction over the issue.

At a cost of at least $14 billion per year, the bill would create a long-term care fund within the $80 billion per-year Medicare program to help pay the costs of lengthy nursing-home stays, home health care, and respite care to relieve unpaid family members or friends who currently provide long-term care for free. Funds for the new program would come from three sources: an increase in premiums beneficiaries already pay for some Medicare services; removal of the $45,000 cap on annual income subject to the 1.45 percent Medicare payroll tax; and imposition of a 5 percent surtax on assets in excess of $200,000 transferred by gift or inheritance.

The most controversial element of the bill was a two-year "exclusionary period"

before Medicare would begin paying the costs for nursing-home care. With nursing-home costs averaging $23,000 per year in 1988, that represented a sizable deductible. Mitchell said he hoped private insurance companies would develop affordable policies to fill in that gap.

Nursing-Home Standards

But while members of Congress debated how to pay for further nursing-home care, they were also expressing concerns about the care being delivered in facilities already receiving federal funds. In fact, during the mid-1980's, a widening consensus emerged that all is not well in many of the nation's nursing homes.

A 1986 report issued by the Institute of Medicine (IoM), the health-sciences arm of the National Academy of Sciences, found that in many of the more than fifteen thousand nursing homes certified to participate in the major federal health programs, "individuals receive very inadequate— sometimes shockingly deficient—care that is likely to hasten the deterioration of their physical, mental and emotional health."

And the General Accounting Office (GAO), in a report released September 16, 1987, by John Heinz of Pennsylvania, ranking Republican on the Senate Special Committee on Aging, found that under the current system of regulations, "nursing homes can remain in the Medicare and Medicaid programs for years with serious deficiencies that threaten patient health and safety."

"Current federal and state systems of inspection and enforcement are incapable of assuring that nursing home residents actually receive the high-quality care the law demands," said Heinz. "The federal government has created a deaf, blind, and mute robot, called it the 'enforcer' and set it loose

Hope for Private-Sector Initiatives ...

A Gallup poll conducted for the American Association of Retired Persons (AARP) in 1984 found that 79 percent of respondents believed—mistakenly—that Medicare pays the bill for long-term care in a nursing home.

Just over half of all nursing-home expenses are paid by the patients themselves or their families. This burden helped increase out-of-pocket health care costs to an estimated 16 percent of the income of elderly Americans in 1986, according to a study by the House Select Committee on Aging. It was the first time out-of-pocket costs topped the 15 percent level since 1965, an event that prompted creation of the Medicare system.

Even with coverage expansions included in the "catastrophic" bill enacted in 1988, Medicare still will pay only for short-term stays (up to 150 days) in skilled-nursing facilities for persons being discharged from hospitals or who are suffering from short-term ailments. It does not cover "custodial" long-term care.

Nor do most "Medigap" policies—private insurance policies that purport to fill in the "gaps" in Medicare coverage. A study by Thomas Rice of the University of North Carolina School of Public Health found that medigap policies "effectively provide no coverage for nursing home care," because they cover only the types of stays also covered by Medicare.

Medicaid, the joint federal-state health plan for the poor, does pay for custodial nursing home care. In 1984, Mediciad footed more than 40 percent of the nation's nursing home bill, to the tune of more than $10 billion. Before it will pay, however, patients must either be poor already or "spend down" their assests to meet the program's strict eligibility standards, which vary from state to state.

Once a person is in a nursing home, that process does not take long. A 1985 study conducted for the House Aging Committee by Massachusetts Blue Cross-Blue Shield found that 63 percent of elderly individuals without a spouse impoverish themselves

with a twig instead of a stick to monitor the nursing home programs."

Demographic Pressures

As medical technology keeps people alive longer and the baby boom generation ages, more Americans than ever before are going to need nursing-home care.

According to the National Center for Health Statistics (NCHS), in 1985 1.3 million of the 1.5 million nursing home residents were over age sixty-five, representing, on any given day, about 5 percent of the

nation's elderly population. By the year 2003, the number of senior citizens who will need nursing home care could rise by as much as 115 percent.

That is because the "old-old," those aged eighty-five and older, are both the fastest-growing group among the elderly and those most likely to need nursing-home care. In 1984, according to the NCHS, 22 percent of those eighty-five and older were in nursing homes, compared with less than 2 percent of those sixty-five to seventy-four.

And while just over half of the annual nursing home bill is paid by patients or their

... to Ease Burden of Long-term Care Costs

after only thirteen weeks in a nursing home. According to the study, 83 percent become impoverished inside a year.

To many public officials, the great hope is private-sector involvement. And the great hope within the private sector is the development of comprehensive, affordable insurance for long-term care. Such policies are already on the market. At least sixteen companies in mid-1986 covered an estimated 100,000 people, according to the Brookings Institution. But that is a tiny fraction of the elderly population.

The biggest problem with marketing the plans, observers agreed, is the widespread perception among the elderly that Medicare already covers nursing-home care. But there are other problems, too, including the reluctance of insurers to develop long-term-care policies. And at an annual premium of $2,000 and up, the policies are too costly for most senior citizens.

Another proposal gaining attention is the "individual medical account," or IMA. This would be a tax-exempt savings account, similar to Individual Retirement Accounts (IRAs), that would provide a hedge against the costs of long-term care.

Other private-sector initiatives include so-called life-care or continuing care communities, and "reverse mortgages." Life-care communities combine the residential units with varying degrees of nursing and other medical services. Although the communities can lower some costs by providing services in a single setting, they are still very expensive, and most limit entry to healthy individuals. Reverse mortgages are designed to enable the elderly who own their own homes to recover some of their equity. Under the concept, an elderly individual sells his or her house, receives a monthly payment, and is allowed to continue living in the house. When the person dies or is institutionalized, the new owner takes possession, with any equity still owed going to the estate. Many elderly, however, are reluctant to part with their homes, the only major asset they may retain and still qualify for Medicaid.

---

families, federal, state, and local governments are not far behind in footing the bill. In 1986, according to the Department of Health and Human Services, patients paid $19.4 billion of the $38.1 billion nursing home tab; the federal government, $10.1 billion ($8.8 billion via the Medicaid program); and state and local governments, $8 billion ($7 billion through Medicaid).

Not a New Problem

The quality problems plaguing "bad apples" in the nursing home industry were nothing new, and neither were federal efforts to address those problems.

For years, Congress heard horror stories about patients forced to lie for days in their own wastes, kept unnecessarily sedated, robbed of their money or personal effects by unscrupulous staffers, or deprived of their right to see visitors.

When Congress created the Medicare and Medicaid programs in 1965, it granted the federal government explicit authority to set standards for nursing homes that wanted to participate in those programs. But in the programs' first year, only 740 of more than

6,000 applying homes could fully meet the established health and safety standards.

Occasional GAO audits as well as studies performed by other agencies show that significant numbers of substandard nursing homes continue to participate in the programs. The GAO report released by Heinz in September 1987 found that more than a third of the facilities in the states sampled failed to meet one or more of the so-called "conditions of participation" for three or more consecutive years.

Two Levels of Care

There are two levels of nursing-home care. So-called skilled-nursing facilities (SNFs), designed for those needing professional nursing care on a daily basis, must meet eighteen separate conditions of participation, including having a licensed nurse on duty twenty-four hours per day. Intermediate-care facilities (ICFs), designed for those who have few or no medical needs but are unable to care for themselves, must meet less stringent requirements. They must have staff on duty twenty-four hours per day, for example, but not necessarily licensed nurses.

More than 9,000 facilities in 1987 were certified by the federal or state governments to provide either skilled care, or both skilled and intermediate care. About 5,300 were certified to provide intermediate care only.

While the federal government sets the standards, each state is responsible for licensing and monitoring facilities within its jurisdiction to ensure compliance. States also inspect facilities participating in the all-federal Medicare program, making recommendations about certification to federal officials. A key reason so many substandard facilities continue to collect government funds, according to both GAO and IoM, is the lack of so-called intermediate sanctions. In most cases, the only action that could be taken against a home with repeated violations was to disqualify it from Medicare or Medicaid participation altogether. But that action punishes patients as much as it does offending nursing homes, because facilities that lose their certification usually close down, leaving patients with no place to go.

The situation was exacerbated by the large number of states that kept tight controls on the number of nursing home beds that could be built in order to keep their Medicaid costs under some sort of control. Even with shortages of nursing home beds in most states, nursing home care for the elderly consumed nearly 39 cents of every Medicaid dollar spent in 1984, though the elderly made up only 14.8 percent of all Medicaid recipients.

Congress in 1981 granted HHS authority to ban payments for new admissions to facilities found to be repeat violators—an intermediate sanction recommended by many experts—but regulations spelling out how that authority is to be applied were not issued in final form until August 1986. And some advocates for the elderly contend that the regulations are too cumbersome and too riddled with loopholes to be of much use.

Thus, said critics, since nursing-home administrators know that regulators were unlikely to impose the "death penalty" of decertification, they had little incentive to remedy even serious problems.

Another oft-cited problem was the regulations' emphasis on a facility's physical ability to provide care. "The regulations do not require assessment of the quality of care being delivered," said the IoM report. "Rather, they require assessment of the facility's structural capacity to provide care."

Not only should regulations be more "patient-oriented," the IoM panel recommended, but all nursing home residents should be given a standard assessment of physical, mental, and social needs upon admittance, and a plan should be drawn up to meet those needs. Such an assessment would both provide a blueprint for care of the patient and give government examiners a better basis for judging the quality of care provided by nursing homes.

Inadequate or undertrained staff is a frequently cited problem, especially in intermediate-care facilities, where as much as 90 percent of the care may be provided by nurses' aides in an effort to keep down costs. According to the IoM report, nurses' aides "in many nursing homes are paid very little, receive relatively little training, are inadequately supervised, and are required to care for more residents than they can serve properly."

Finally, even in facilities that can and do meet patients' physical needs, mental and social needs may remain unaddressed— a serious problem, according to the IoM panel. "Because most nursing home residents live in nursing homes for many months or years, quality of life is as important as quality of care in these institutions," said the IoM report.

Legislative Action

HR 3545 (PL 100-203), a 1987 deficit-reduction bill, incorporated a compromise version of legislation (HR 2270, S 1108) rewriting and toughening the rules for nursing homes that participate in Medicare and Medicaid.

Among other things, HR 3545 imposed strict new staffing and training requirements for the nursing homes certified to participate in Medicare and Medicaid. For the first time, nurses' aides, who in most homes provided patients with the bulk of their care, would be required to undergo at least seventy-five hours of training and pass a competency evaluation before being allowed to care for patients. And, beginning in 1990, all nursing homes would be required to have a licensed nurse on duty twenty-four hours per day seven days per week.

In a major setback for House conferees, however, the final package included a Senate provision allowing states to waive the staffing requirement if a nursing home, despite "diligent efforts," cannot find enough qualified staff. The federal government could usurp the state waiver authority, but only after determining by "a clear pattern and practice" that the state has abused its waiver discretion.

Senate conferees argued that the waiver provision was needed because a nationwide shortage of nurses could make it extremely difficult for nursing homes to meet the nurse-staffing requirement. House conferees said they feared states would be too quick to approve such waivers in an effort to circumvent the new rules.